Flat and Office are an integral part of today's metropolitan life because most of the time of the metropolitan people is spent in flat and office. Positive energy affects life as well as working efficiency hence flat & office should be constructed as per the Vaastu & Feng Shui. The learned auther has explained, in detail, a scientific study of Vaastu & Feng Shui for happy and prosperous life in this book.

VAASTU, FENG SHUI

Flat & Office

Vaasṭu Guru

Kuldeep Saluja

FUSION BOOKS

ISBN - 81-8419-044-1

Publisher	:	**Fusion Books** X-30, Okhla Industrial Area, Phase-II, New Delhi-110020.
Phone	:	011-41611861
Fax	:	011-41611866
E-mail	:	sales@diamondpublication.com
Website	:	www.diamondpublication.com
Edition	:	2007

Vaastu, Feng Shui–*Flat & Office*
By Vaastu Guru Kuldeep Saluja

DEDICATION

This book is dedicated to

my respected Parents

(Late) Sardar Tara Singh Ji Dhoul

and

(Late) Smt. Rampyari Dhoul.

PREFACE

Vaastushaastra is an old science. It is related to universal truth and not any religion or cult. After research for thousands of years our *rishi-munis* have made it useful for common people.

Vaastushaatra is very significant in today's lifestyle. In present times if anything goes wrong in the life of a person then, in addition to all other factors he also thinks about Vaastu defects at his residence and/or office. It is due to this increasing popularity of Vaastushaastra that every Tom, Dick and Harry is now *Vaastushaastri* these days. Interestingly you will find that some of them even do not know how to look at compass properly. These *Vaastushaastris* have created their own remedies to remove Vaastu defects, e.g. to plant *tulsi* in front of house, to tie a cow in front of house, to bury a pyramid in the earth or on the door, to put *'Yantra'* in copper plate, to put God's idol or Shri Yantra etc.

Vaastushaastra is a medium to take advantage of energy present in the nature by coordinating with the same. Nowadays Vaastushaastra has become a fashion and due to this it is practised more as a superstition and less on scientific basis.

I regularly write on Vaastu in the famous magazine *'Grihlaxmi'* and receive a lot of mail from my readers. I made up my mind to write on this science of construction (Building) after receiving my readers' mail. I wanted to help them to solve their Vaastu problems in a scientific way. I also wanted to remove their illusion, about Vaastu and to save them from the cheating done by many of the so-called *Vaastushaastris*.

I have studied books on Vaastu by learned *Vaastushaastris* like Sri B.N. Reddy, Sri Dronam Raju, Puranchandra Rao and

Sri R.G. Rao. This inspired me to write and unveil many mysteries of the subject. I am indebted to them.

I would like to extend my special thanks to Dr. Rashmi Ramdhoni, Associate Prof. Head of the Hindi Department, Mahatma Gandhi Institute, Mauritius, who translated my articles on Vaastu in French. These were published in the *"Week End"*, the main newspaper of Mauritius media.

I extend my thanks to Shri Sanjay Sharma for translating this work into English.

I am indebted to my wife Smt. Kuldeep Saluja, daughters-in-law, Sheetal and Rashmi, for their loving support.

Last but not the least, I extend my gratitude to Sri Narendra Kumar Varma (Publisher and Director, Diamond books) for his encouragement, which has enabled me to put my deep study and research in the form of this book.

–Kuldeep Saluja
Vaastu Guru

CONTENTS

UNIVERSAL VAASTUSHAASTRA AND FENG SHUI

Vaastushaastra and Feng shui both are old sciences of India and China to coordinate between buildings or shape of land, proportions and direction with the environment of their surroundings. Vaastu affects houses, shops, factories, schools, hospitals, *dharamshalas*, public offices, religious places, rivers, crematoria, casinos, bars, brothels etc. and even roads, squares, three roads, streets, towns, cities, i.e. everyplace on earth equally.

These days when somebody constructs his house he takes utmost care to decorate its outer and inner sides. He also takes care to get maximum comforts in the house, but he never seriously thinks whether his new house will provide him happiness, prosperity, fame, health and peace or not. If you are living in a place but do not get mental peace, good health, family is distressed and under pressure, you go through all types of troubles continuously. Do you think that there is any use in living in such a place?

Vaastushaastra was invented after continuous research by our *rishi–munis* to provide happy life and to save all of us from troubles of life in the world. The principles of Vaastushaastra are completely according to the principles of nature.

All the ancient palaces, temples and towns which were constructed as per the Vaastu principles are still shining, e.g. Tirupati Balaji Temple of Andhra Pradesh, Badrinath Temple, Maa Vaishnodevi Temple, Taj Mahal, Temples of Khajuraho, and Jaipur city etc. The buildings that were not constructed as per the Vaastu principles are nowhere to be seen now.

We can experience the examples of Vaastu around us. Sometimes we feel happy on entering the house of a friend and there is an inner feeling to go there again and again. On the other hand, in some other house the moment we enter a sort of suffocating feeling comes in our heart and we do not wish to go there again. Similarly, we find that a tenant in a certain house in our neighborhood succeeds in every field of life and then constructs a house of his own and shifts to the same, whereas there is a house wherein if anybody stays he is always in trouble. All the family members remain troubled financially, physically and mentally and one day they leave the house. Some people construct extravagant house with all the modern facilities and live there, but later on they die without any kids and that house is ruined. Many factory owners face labour problems, governmennt raids, accidents etc. in the initial stage itself and they finally close the same. On the other hand, there are examples of people who had humble beginnings, got success rapidly, increased their business manifold, became rich and lived a happy and prosperous life.

If a hut is constructed as per Vaastu then the residents do not face much trouble for their daily needs. The family progresses and gradually becomes prosperous. Opposite to this if a bungalow is not constructed as per Vaastu the residents of the same have to struggle even for daily needs, no matter how rich they are. They gradually lose their social status and prosperity. Their lives become miserable due to continuous physical, mental and financial problems. There are certain "Vaastu-defects", which are to be eradicated immediately as they start affecting very soon.

While applying Vaastu the importance is given to the house in which you live no matter whether you are an owner or a tenant or even it could be a temporary or permanent place of your stay. Vaastu is applicable everywhere. Suppose you are sailing in a boat and there is a hole at the bottom of the same, now it is almost certain that you will be drown but the fact that the boat owner is somebody else and you only boarded it to cross the river does not change its result.

The Vaastu consultant has to be especially sensitive towards two things– first, the needs of those living in the premises and second, the requirement of the same premises. It is because the house is for those who live in. An able Vaastu consultant is one who coordinates between the Vaastu principles and available resources of a premises.

THE INDIAN VAASTUSHAASTRA

The fundamentals of the Indian Vaastushaastra are five universal five elements, i.e. earth, water, fire, wind and sky. Our body and the whole universe are made up of these five elements.

Vaastu is basically to construct and decorate our house as per these five elements. Vaastu is a science which guides us to take maximum advantage of the magnetic effect present in earth and solar energy. It creates such an effect that by the use of positive and negative solar energy in right proportion we get happiness, peace, prosperity and fame. If you coordinate with three elements viz. earth, water and fire out of the five, the wind and sky are automatically coordinated.

THE CHINESE FENG SHUI AND VAASTUSHAASTRA

Feng Shui is Chinese Vaastushaastra. It is almost 5000 years old science of China. Its meaning is wind and water. In any building if there is right balance between these two then the positive energy is increased and it produces happiness, peace and prosperity. As per the Feng Shui principle, the fortune of a man is of three types:

1. **Fortune From Heaven** : The fortune, which the man gets from his past birth and deeds.
2. **Fortune Created by Man** : This is the fortune which the man creates by his deeds. It is also called his hard earned fortune.
3. **Fortune From Earth** : This is due to the shape, proportion, direction and environment of the house and office etc.

As per Feng Shui there are two types of energies in nature–one is positive and another is negative. The positive energy is called YIN and the negative YANG. Feng Shui coordinates between Yin and Yang in such a way that they are useful for human beings to get happiness, prosperity, mental peace and good health etc.

Yin & Yang

FORTUNE AND VAASTU

Nothing is superior to the fortune. If the fortune of a person is strong and Vaastu is bad even then he gets success but it's after hard work and struggle. If fortune and Vaastu both are strong the person gets success easily and without any struggle. The troubled time of a person passes easily if the fortune is weak and Vaastu is strong, but if fortune and Vaastu both are weak then it is very difficult for that person to cope with the bad times.

It is true that nobody can change the fortune by merely changing the directions but by doing so one can get a bit of relief too. People may say that if the fortune cannot be changed then why we should waste our time in Vaastu.

I would like to give you one example, suppose you fall ill then why do you visit to your doctor? Why don't you simply sit and wait to get well. If you are destined to get well, you will live. But you go to see your doctor and get proper medicines. Similarly, if due to weak fortune you are suffering from physical, mental and financial problems, then you can get some relief by Vaastu. Certainly, we can lead a happy life by just rearranging some things as per Vaastu.

FAITH AND VAASTU

All the civilizations of the world have their religious symbols. In India also we have *Swastika, Om, Shree, Panchgulak Hand,* 786, *Omkar* etc. People have faith in different types of *yantras* too e.g. 'Lakshmi Yantra', 'Shree Yantra', 'Kuber Yantra', 'Kaali Yantra' and 'Surya Yantra' etc.

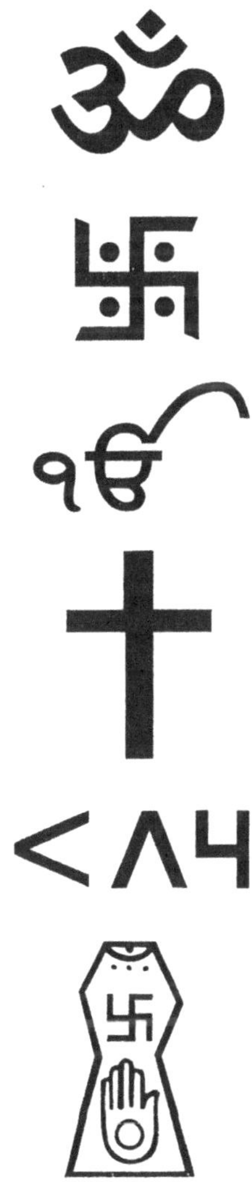

Most of the intellectuals think that only superstitious and idle people wear amulet, *rudraksh*, rings and *yantras* etc. but on the contrary it is true wearing them is very useful. A research has been done by Prof. Richard Wisemen and his scholars of Heartfordshire University, England on the benefits of wearing rings and *rudraksh* etc. religious symbols. They claim to have found corrected destiny of people after wearing these symbols.

Certainly the use of religious symbols and *yantras* develops the positive thinking. People become optimistic about their future. The user of these symbols gets rid of disappointment and develops self-confidence. By the inspiration of self-confidence the person works hard to get success.

These religious symbols are in frequent use to eradicate Vaastu defects in our country. 'Shri Yantra', 'Swastik yantra', 'Vaastu defects eradication Yantra', 'Sawastika', 'Pyramid', 'Siddha Ganapati' and 'Panchmukhi Hanuman' etc. are some of the religious symbols in use. Some Chinese religious symbols such as laughing Buddha, double happiness symbol, Fuk-Luk and Sau, three legged frog and lucky coin are also in use in addition to the Indian religious symbols. These symbols whether proved or not, are not very much useful to eradicate Vaastu defects. When a doctor treats some serious ailment of a patient he usually prescribes some vitamins etc. in addition to the actual medicines. These religious symbols are like vitamin tablets, which do not eradicate Vaastu defects.

As vitamin tablets cannot eradicate a disease, similarly, Vaastu defects also cannot be corrected by using religious symbols. We have to make alterations and modifications in the building to eradicate significant Vaastu defects.

We can explain it by an example, suppose in a building the main gate is in the corner of the "south west zone" and there is an underground water tank, well or bore-well near that main gate, then there is maximum possibility of unnatural death of one of the male family members. If you want to correct this Vaastu defect by using any of the religious symbols, it will definitely not work. This Vaastu defect can only be corrected by closing this gate and constructing a new gate in west of the north-west and the underground water source has also to be closed by soil filling.

We can understand the significance of the removal of Vaastu defect by the following example. If we put zero after 1 then it becomes 10. Again by putting one more zero we can make it 100. So by putting one zero we can increase the value of a digit ten times. But if the digit 1 is not there then there is no value of a zero. So all the changes made in a building as per Vaastu are like a digit if we put religious symbols they increase the effect of changes made, but symbol alone can not be effective.

VAASTUSHAASTRA IS A SCIENCE

The principles of Vaastushaastra are fully scientific. We can prove it by analyzing some of them.

1. **Water in North-East Zone :** If the water source is in the north-east zone then all the bacteria etc. present in the water are destroyed by morning sun rays. This fact is also confirmed by science.
2. **Courtyard in the East:** It is recommended to get sunbath and maximum exposure to sun rays in the morning. It is supposed to be very useful for health.
3. **Tree in the East:** Big trees are not to be grown in the east of the house as they obstruct the positive morning sun rays from entering the house.
4. **Kitchen in the South-East Zone:** If the kitchen of the house is in the south-east zone the morning sun rays enter the kitchen from east, which destroy bacteria and germs in food.
5. **High and Thick Walls in the West:** The morning sun rays are useful. They give advantage but when the sun is in the west, at the time of noon, the sun rays are harmful. Vaastushaastra suggests us to construct high and thick walls in the south-west to protect us from these harmful sun rays.
6. **Head in South Direction While Sleeping:** Our head works as the North Pole and legs as the South Pole. If we keep our head in north direction while sleeping, then there will be a distraction due to the North Pole of the earth.

This will create a tension and disturb sleep. That's why Vaastushaastra suggests us to keep our head in south while sleeping. This will give us sound sleep and good health.

Thus many scientific logics prove the principles of Vaastushaastra. Hence we should remove the Vaastu defects scientifically only. Whenever there is a Vaastu defect it cannot be removed or corrected by any charm, *puja* or religious symbol. If the Vaastu of a temple is defective then people are not attracted towards the same while the God himself sits in the temple.

Vaastushaastra and Feng Shui help us in improving every field of the life. Removal of Vaastu defects of the house and office, etc. with the help of Vaastushaastra and Feng Shui produces wonderful results. That's why this centuries old oriental science is fast becoming popular in the West too.

IMPROTANCE OF THE SUN IN VAASTU

The whole universe gets life from the sun. In fact, the sun is the base of the universe. East direction is the way through which we get the positive energy of the sun. That is why east and north are two very significant directions as per Vaastu. The energy of the sun enters any house or building from north-east zone only and the space energy also enters the same way. A special energy region is produced by the fusion of these two energies. This gives positive results to the inhabitants.

Man is aware of vital power of the sun. From the beginning various civilizations have worshipped the sun. This proves vital importance of the sun.

The morning sun rays possess many advantageous things– this has been proved by science also. Our skins absorb vitamin D from these sun rays. The white sun rays actually consist of seven colours i.e. violet, indigo, blue, green, yellow, orange and red. All these colours affect our health. Colour and naturopathy use sun rays. These sun rays destroy germs and bacteria.

The morning sun rays are best due to their less temperature and more light. That's why the Vaastushaastra recommends keeping more space, doors and windows in the east so that more and more sun rays enter the house and the courtyard. This destroys the bacteria and germs and produces healthy environment for a healthy life. Good health is the biggest wealth.

REMEDIES OF VAASTUSHAASTRA AND FENG SHUI AND THEIR LIMITATIONS

There are various points and effective remedies to remove Vaastu defects of any building in the Indian Vaastushaastra. Most of these remedies require demolition of certain construction and then new construction as per Vaastu. For example a toilet in the north-east zone is inauspicious as per Vaastu. Hence it is removed from there and constructed at some other appropriate place. If bore well or other underground water source is not in the north-east zone then it is fully closed and constructed in the north-east zone.

Chinese Vaastushaastra– Feng Shui– says that if there is a problem there is a remedy. Feng Shui uses some external and internal remedies to remove some small Vaastu defects. The following list gives an idea about the things used to remove Vaastu defects by Feng Shui.

Light and things reflect light, living things, comfortable sounds, moving things, mechanical things, water, plants and colours etc.

PYRAMID AND VAASTU

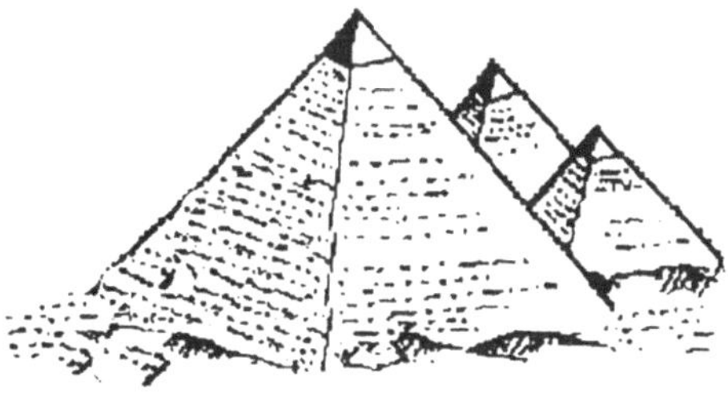

The pyramids are tombs of the Pharaohs or kenps of ancient Egypt on the banks of the Nile River. These are about four thousand years old. These were constructed as per Vaastu in a straight line of the Pole Star in the sky in north direction. The pyramid structures are really unique example of Vaastu and medicinal specialty. Taking the inspiration from the pyramids of Egypt many experiments were performed in various countries of the world. In one such experiment a dead body was kept in the pyramid and amazingly the body did not decay. Mr. Bowis, a French investigator, was amazed to find that inside the pyramid when a rat or cat died no bad smell was produced. The body mummified, dried and did not decay. He could not find any plausible explanation for this whole phenomenon. After a lot of thinking he concluded that this might be due to the shape of the pyramid. For the confirmation of this he prepared a small pyramid and put a dead cat in the same. He was surprised to find that the cat did not decay and was mummified. He then experimented with other perishable things like vegetables and milk.

He found that these things remained fresh for about a week. He kept rubbish beneath the pyramid and found that this too dried without any bad smell. This gave birth to a new science that the geometrical shapes are deeply related to life energies. Now Bowis suggests that all the hospitals should be constructed in the pyramid shape so that the patients get well soon. Many experiments have been done on this concept. If a wound is kept inside the pyramid shape it heals faster. Similarly toothache, headache etc. are relieved faster when kept beneath the pyramid shape.

Pyramid word consist of a Greek word 'Pyre' = fire and 'Mid' = centre. So the meaning of the word is that pyramid is a place that has fire (energy) at its centre. It is this energy that keeps things fresh inside it. For centuries temples, mosques, churches, *gurudwaras*, Bodh *matts* etc. have been constructed with upper shape as a dome, which is a kind of pyramid only. We get fresh air and peace if we sit beneath these dome shaped structures. It gives us mental happiness and concentration due to a special energy that flows through this pyramid (dome) shape. In short, we can say that a pyramid is an equipment to store energy. Pyramids are useful in medicine and meditation but they are not useful to remove Vaastu defects.

In Egypt also, where pyramids were invented, they were used to keep dead bodies safe. The world renowned Feng Shui practitioner, Lilian Too, has also described the misuse of the pyramids in Vaastu defects. In China, from where Feng Shui originated, pyramids are not used to remove Vaastu defects.

Note: Please read *"Vaastu & Feng Shui for Better Health"* by the same author to know the misuse of pyramid in removing Vaastu defects.

SHREE YANTRA AND VAASTU

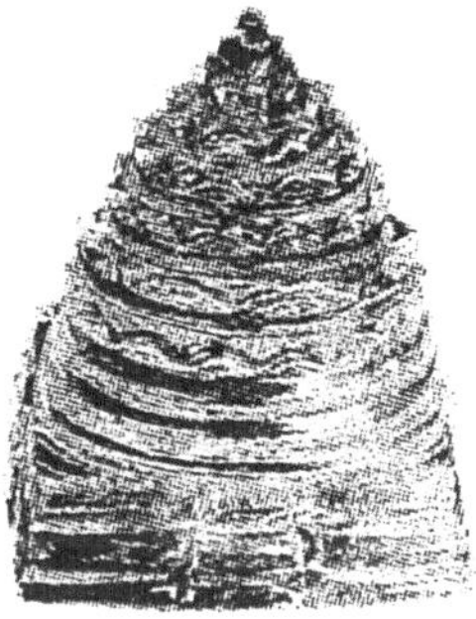

Shree Yantra has religious importance no matter whether proved or not. It may be made up of quartz or any other metal but has no use in removal of Vaastu defects. Here I want to clear one thing that the quartz Shree Yantra may be religiously important but quartz circles have their own use in removal of Vaastu defects. The quartz circle works as a prism, reflects light which has a scientific basis. These circles are used to attract more natural light through window, when placed in front of window panes. Cuts of these circles reflect more light to make the place full of energy.

Note: To know the misuse of the Shree Yantra in detail, please read *"Vaastu & Feng Shui for Happiness & Prosperity"* by the same author.

DETERMINATION OF DIRECTION IN VAASTUSHAASTRA AND FENG SHUI

A magnetic compass is used to determine the directions in the Indian Vaastushaastra. While determining the Vaastu disposition of a building the magnetic compass is kept at the centre of the building. The Vaastu defect of the building can only be removed by this direction determination.

The Chinese Feng Shui uses two methods. First is the use of "Luo Pan", the Chinese compass. Auspicious and inauspicious directions are determined on the basis of the date of birth in this method. The second method is based on magic square called – Pa Kua. Every Vaastu is divided into eight parts in it based on the main gate of the building or the door of the room. In this method, the north direction is always there where the gate is.

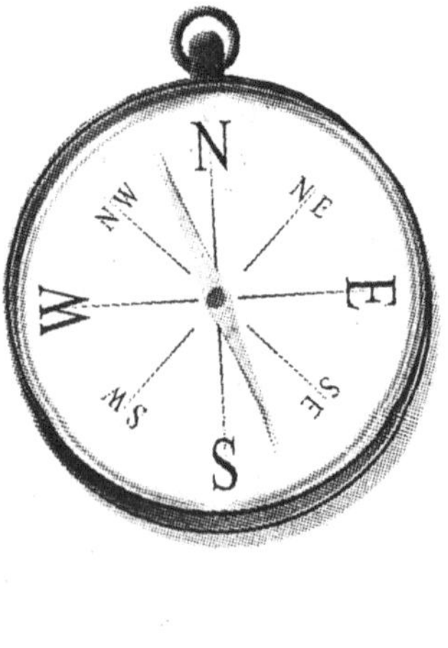

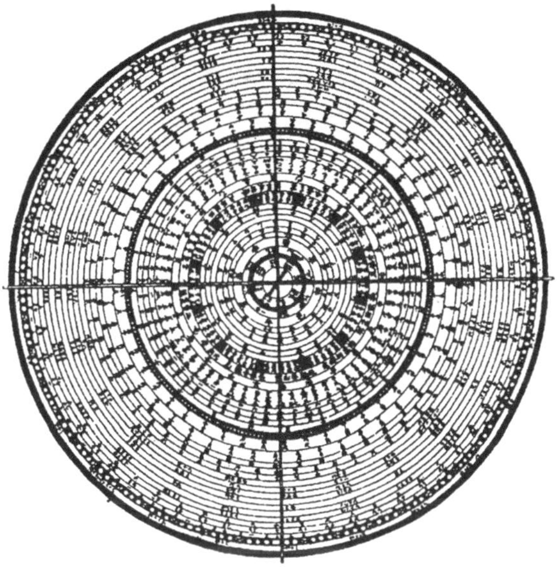

Chinese Compass Luo Pan

No compass is used in the Pa Kua method. Many small problems could be removed by just applying this method. This method is currently very popular in India.

Nine Planets Affecting Eight Directions

As per the Indian Vaastushaastra the nine planets present in our solar system affect all the eight directions of a plot or building. Every planet represents one direction as below:

DIRECTION PLANET

ENGLISH	HINDI	ENGLISH	HINDI
East	*Purva*	Sun	*Surya*
South	*Dakshin*	Mars	*Mangal*
West	*Paschim*	Saturn	*Shani*
North	*Uttar*	Mercury	*Budh*
South-East	*Agneya*	Venus	*Shukr*
South-West	*Nairitya*	Rahu	*Rahu*
North-West	*Vayavya*	Moon	*Chandrma*
North- East	*Ishaan*	Jupiter/Ketu	*Guru/Ketu*

DIRECTIONS AND ANGLES AS PER VAASTUSHAASTRA

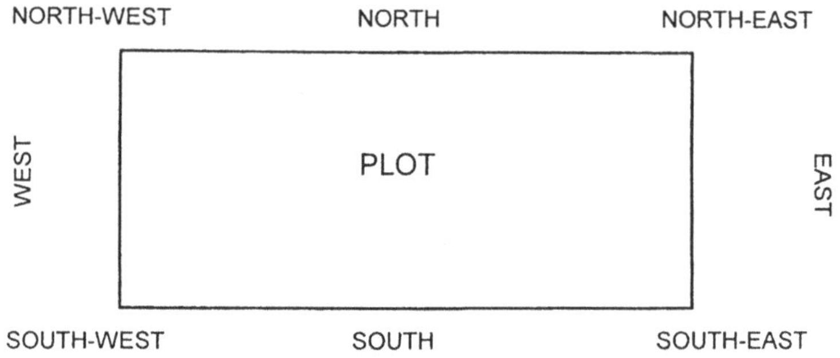

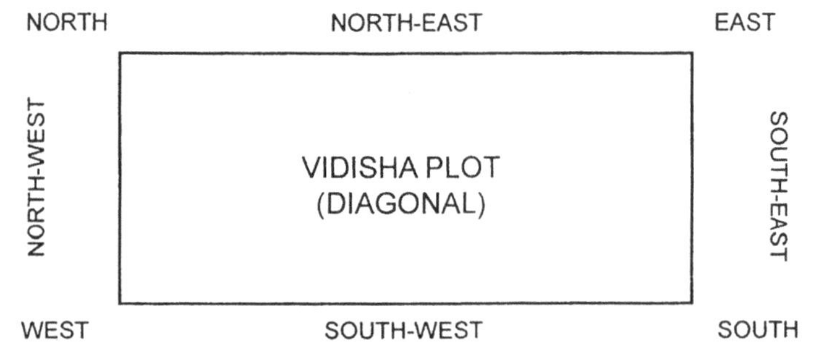

"A plot which has directions at the corners is called a "VIDISHA PLOT(DIAGONAL)".

FOUR DIRECTIONS

East	*Purva*	– Direction of sunrise.
West	*Pashchim*	– Direction of sunset.
North	*Uttar*	– Direction of the North Pole.
South	*Dakshina*	– Direction of the South Pole.

FOUR ANGLES

North-East	*Ishaan*	– Direction in between north and east.
South-East	*Agneya*	– Direction in between east and south.
South-West	*Nairutya*	– Direction in between west and south.
North-West	*Vayavya*	– Direction in between west and north.

DIVISION OF PLOT

Division of plot in eight parts as per Vaastu.

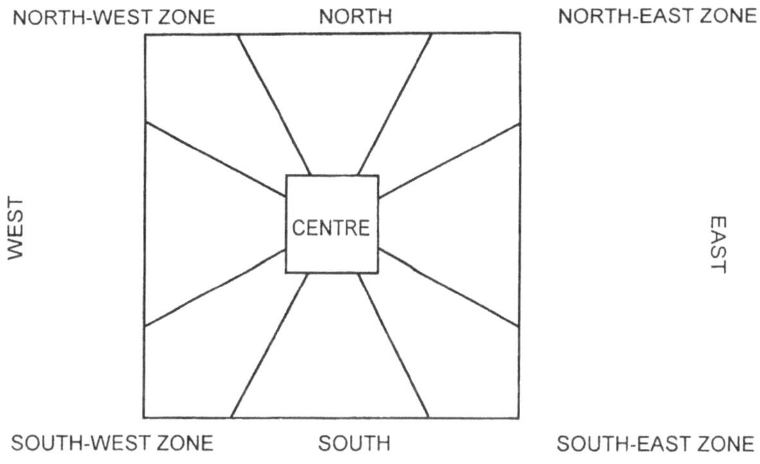

Division of a VIDISHA (Diagonal) plot as per Vaastu

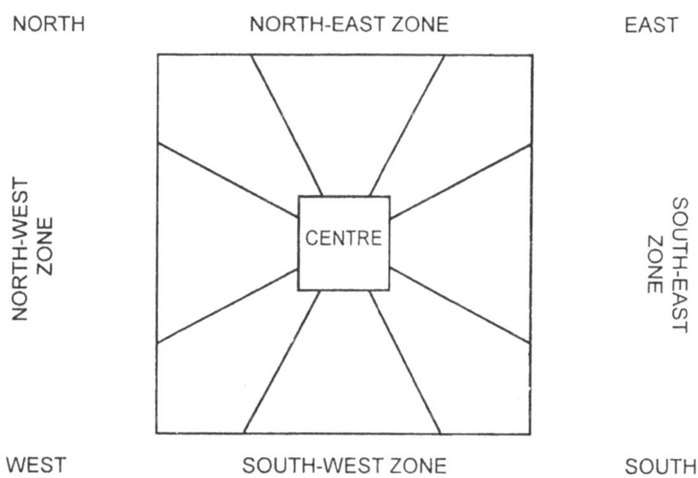

The centre point is called *"Brahma sthan"* in Vaastushaastra.

DIVISION OF VAASTU IN EIGHT PARTS AS PER FENG SHUI

	SE	SOUTH	SW	
	Wealth & Good Luck	Fame Recognition	Marriage Relation	
EAST	Elders, Family Seniors	Earth, Health	Children, Creativity	WEST
	Knowledge	Career & Opportunity	Helpful Friends	
	NE	NORTH	NW	

Main gate could be anywhere in this direction.

As per the magic square Pa-kua system of Feng Shui, a plot/building/room can be divided into eight parts. The direction of the main gate is always north.

FLAT–VAASTU AND FENG SHUI

Everyone has a dream of a small and beautiful house. Less land is available due to increasing population of the cities and metros and this is the reason behind very high rates of the plots. Builders want to use every inch of the plot for financial benefit and in this greed they do not follow the principles of Vaastushaastra in multi-storeyed buildings. If a person chooses to purchase and live in a flat of such a building his life becomes miserable.

A Gujarati family happily residing in the Borivli area of Mumbai purchased a flat in a near by multi-storeyed building. The flat was not as per the Vaastu and they faced many problems even in the first year. Their income reduced. Women of the family fell ill. Their son who, always stood first in all exams, somehow passed that year. The flat had a cut in its north-east direction and this was its main Vaastu defect. There was an underground water tank in the west-south-west direction.

By merely keeping account of the following small but very important Vaastu principles, while purchasing a flat, one can lead a happy and healthy life successfully.

- The multi-storeyed building in which the flat is situated should be on a square or rectangular plot. Corner of the south-west zone of the plot should be of 90^0. There should be much more open space in the north-east zone . The residents of the flat on such a plot are happy and prosperous.

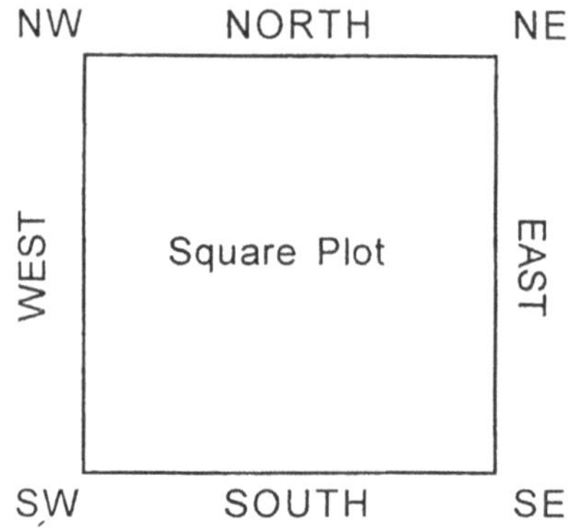

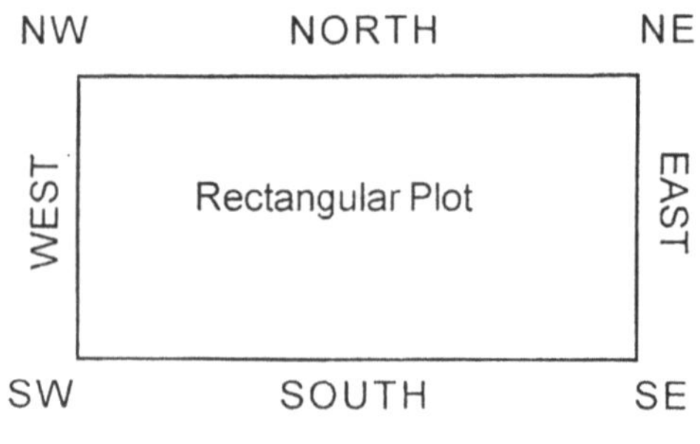

- Purchase a flat in such a building, which has deep pits, ponds and rivers etc. in north-east and hillocks in the south-west. A flat in such a building will be a boon for you.

- Do not purchase a flat in a building which has high buildings, hills, rocks or big trees such as *pipal*, banyan tree etc. in the north-east zone and deep pits, ponds and rivers etc. in the south-west zone. Such a flat is prone to problems.

- Do not purchase a flat in the building near which there are trees of long roots such as *pipal*, banyan tree, mango, tamarind etc. Long and deep roots of such trees are harmful to the building.
- Do not purchase a plot near a drain. The bad smell of the same makes life difficult and health problem also arise.
- Do not purchase a plot near high-tension line.The electromagnetic rays of these wire create health problem. Similarly, do not purchase plot near a transformer.

- Construct your building in square or rectangle shape after leaving maximum open space in the north and east directions at right angle, for good fortune.

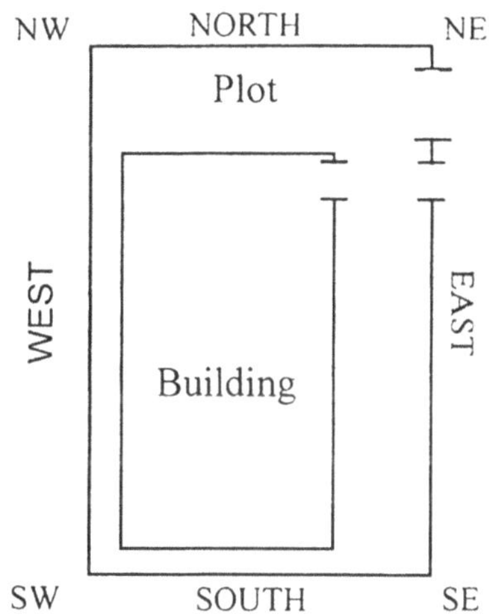

Ideal condition of building construction on a plot

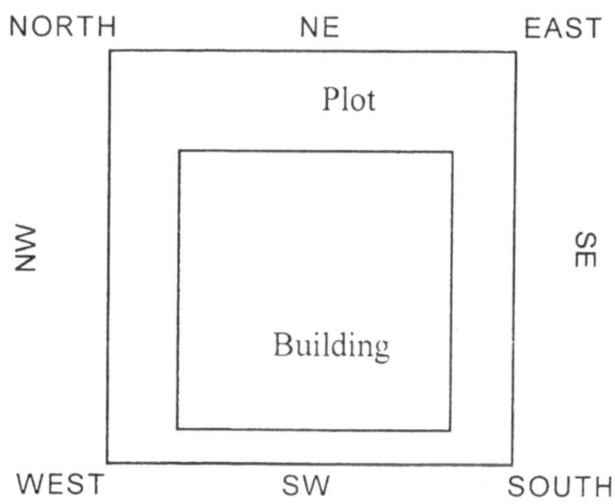

Ideal condition of multi-storeyed building construction on a *Vidisha* plot.

- If the north, east and north-east zones are down, cut or round then it is inauspicious. This causes financial burden and brings bad name to the family. If these directions are increased its very auspicious. To remove the above defects these directions should be right-angled.

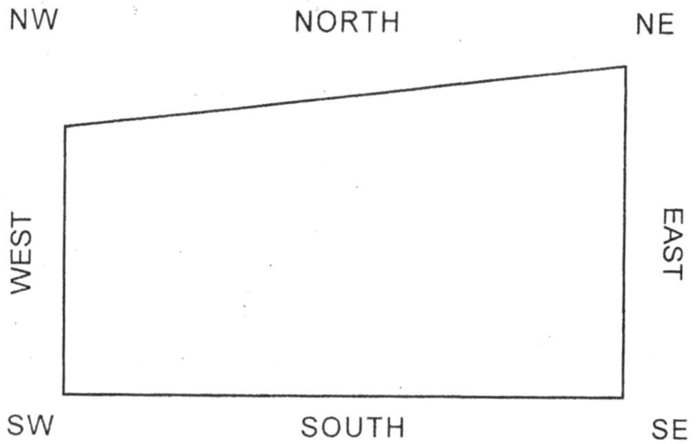

North of the north-east direction auspicious flat

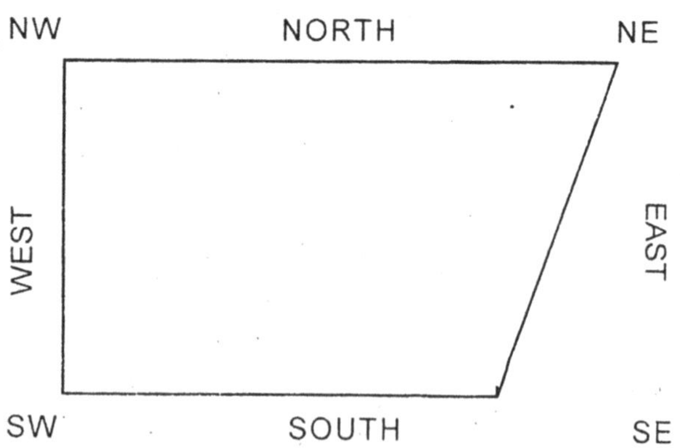

East of the north-east direction auspicious flat

- Out of all the eight directions the north-east zone is very important. Care must be taken about all the Vaastu principles for this zone. Purchase flat in such a building, which has an underground water tank, well, bore well or swimming pool in north, north-east or east direction. If these things are in any other direction, they produce devastating results.
- The north, north-east and eastern part of the plot on which a multi-storeyed building is constructed, should be on the lower side than the south, south western and west part. A flat in such a building can be purchased. If the north-east is higher, it is inauspicious and brings ill fate to the family.

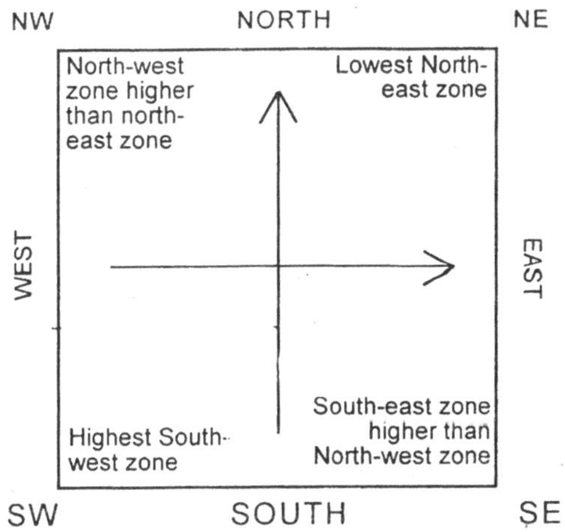

High and low of the plot as per Vaastu

- If the multi-storeyed building is east or south facing then its main gate should be on left side. If it is west or north facing then the main gate should on right side. In both these conditions it's auspicious. As per the figure the entrance to the building should only be on the right mark places. If it is through the crossed places then it brings troubles in the life.

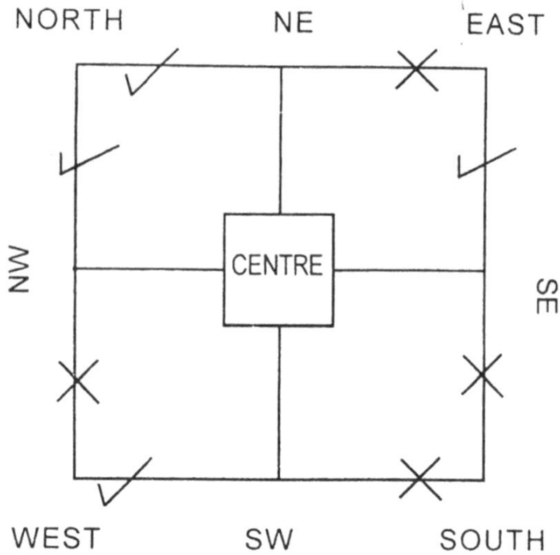

Main gate as per Vaastu

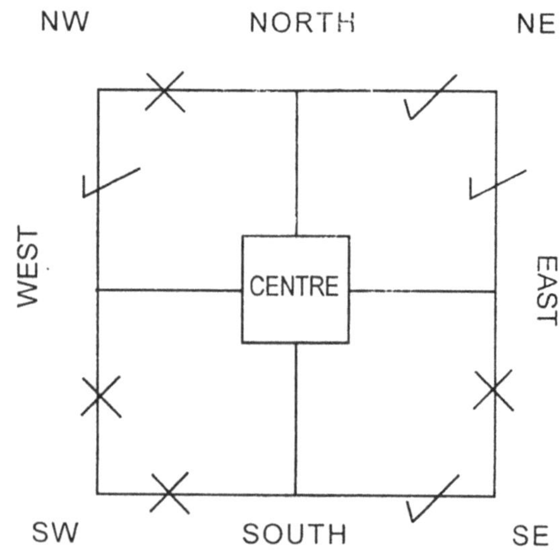

Main gate as per Vaastu in a *VIDISHA* Plot

VITHISHULA (T-Junction)

- When a public road stops in front of a plot or a multi-storeyed building or enters straight into the plot, it is called *VITHISHULA*. Some of these are auspicious and others inauspicious.

Auspicious *Vithishula*

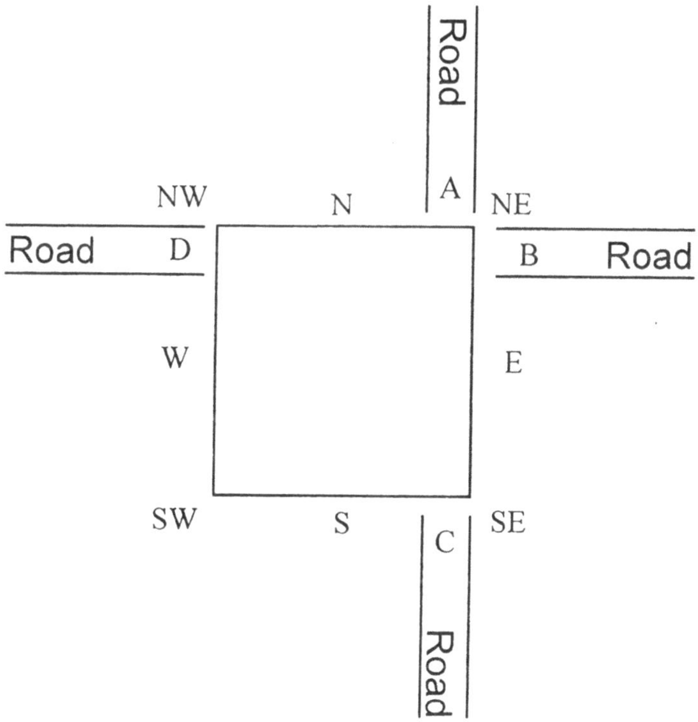

Figure - 1

There are four auspicious *Vithishula* as in the figure(1)

(A) *Vithishula* entering from the north of the north-east.

(B) *Vithishula* entering from the east of the north-east.

(C) *Vithishula* entering from the south of the south-east.

(D) *Vithishula* entering from the west of the north-west.

- People living in a flat of a building with an inauspicious *vithishula*, lead miserable and troubled lives.

Inauspicious *Vithishula*

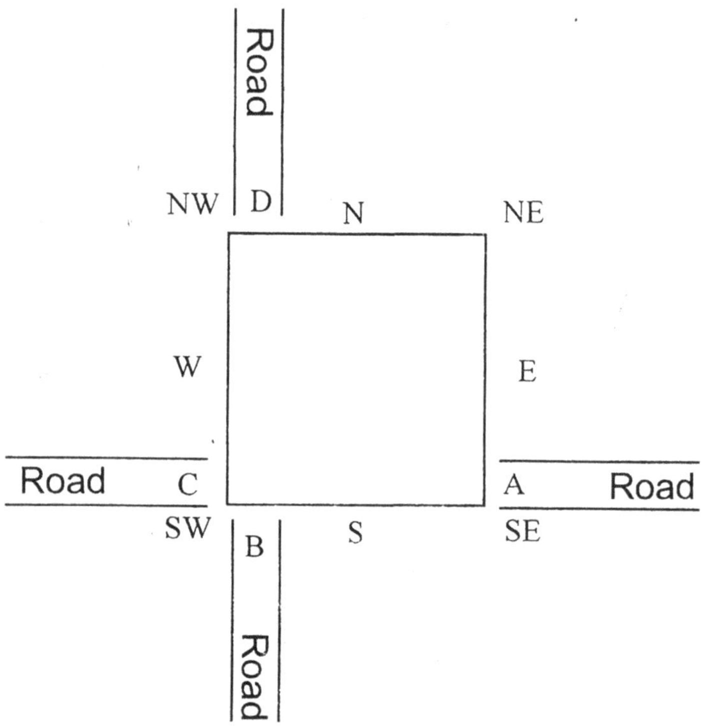

Figure - 2

Figure 2 : Shows four inauspicious *Vithishulas:*

(A) *Vithishula* entering from the east of the south-east.

(B) *Vithishula* entering from the south of the south-west.

(C) *Vithishula* entering from the west of the south-west.

(D) *Vithishula* entering from the north of the north-west.

- A hurdle in front of the main gate of the building it is called Vedh (penetration) e.g. electricity pole, pillar, tree, open drain and edged corner of other building. This is inauspicious and brings ill fate. This defect is not considered when these hurdles are on a distance double of the height of the building. If there is a public road in between the hurdle and the building then this defect is removed. Similarly, if the hurdle is in left or right of the building the defect is not counted for.

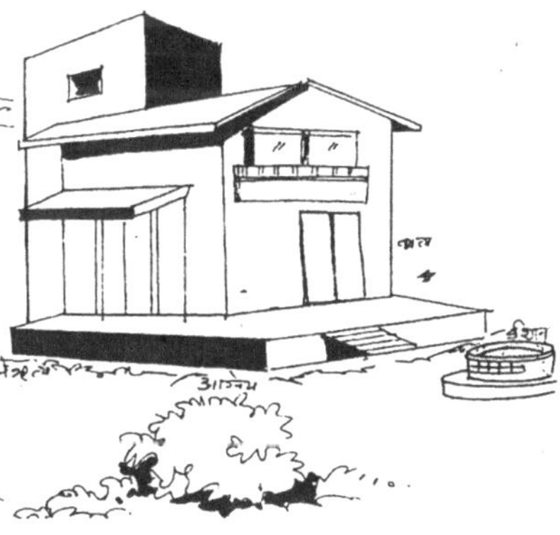

- The multi-storeyed building should never be on a T-junction. People living in a building on T- junction face miserable accidents.

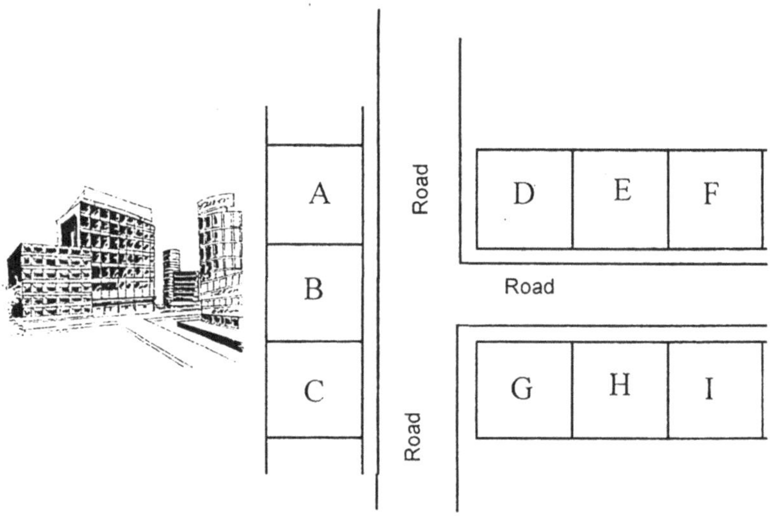

Plot "B" is on T- junction

- A plot situated in front of two or more roads is not suitable for a multi-storeyed building. No matter if such a plot is square or rectangular in shape people staying in the flats of such a building can never be happy.

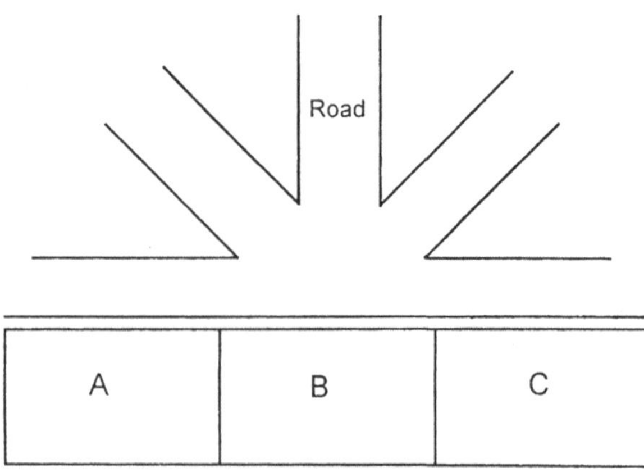

Plot "B" is inauspicious due to more than two roads.

- Plot situated at the "V" joint is not suitable for a multi-storeyed building. Residents of the flats in a multi-storeyed building on such a plot are always in troubles.

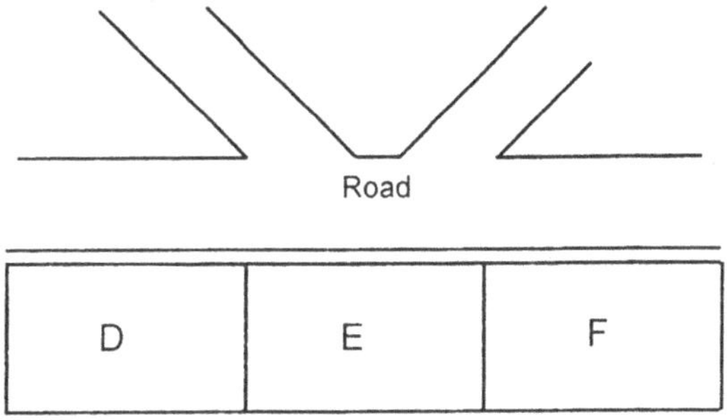

Plot 'E' at the 'V' Junction

- Any plot situated on a sharp turn is also not advisable for a multi-storeyed building. Residents of such a building never succeed in any field of life.

Plot situated on sharp turn.

One unsafe tall building among tiny buildings

- Please bear in mind that any building which is either too high or too low than other buildings surrounding it, is not safe for living. If there is a higher building behind a building, it is auspicious.
- Do not even think of purchasing a flat in the place in front of which there is a high building or another construction. If there is a high building behind that place then it is auspicious.

- Purchase of flats is not advisable, at all, in the multi-storeyed building on either side of a dead end. In fact, dead ends do not give way to energy and hence the residents do not get happiness.

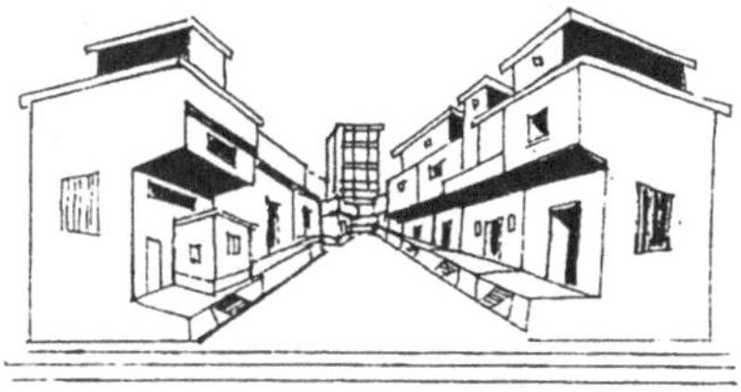

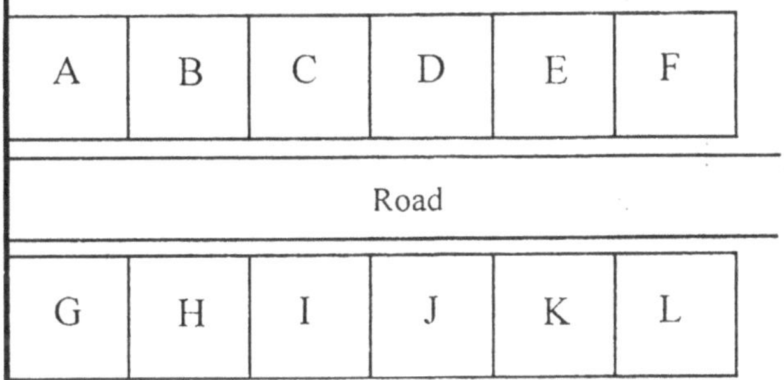

Plot A & G are inauspicious because of dead end.

ROADS AROUND MULTI-STOREYED BUILDING

A multi-storeyed building along with four parallel roads around it is auspicious. A person living in a flat of such a building progresses well and possesses good health, prosperity and fame. The *Aashram* of mother Teresa situated at Kolkata is its best example.

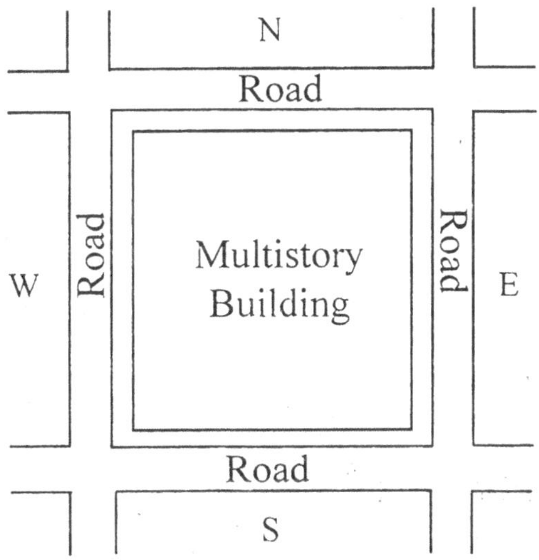

Roads around a multi-storeyed building

A. If there are roads in more than one direction of a multi-storeyed building, it is auspicious.
B. Roads in the north-east zone yield good health and prosperity.
C. Roads in the south and north direction are auspicious for ladies.
D. Roads in the south and west directions are auspicious for businessmen.
E. Roads in the north and west directions give prosperity and fame to all.

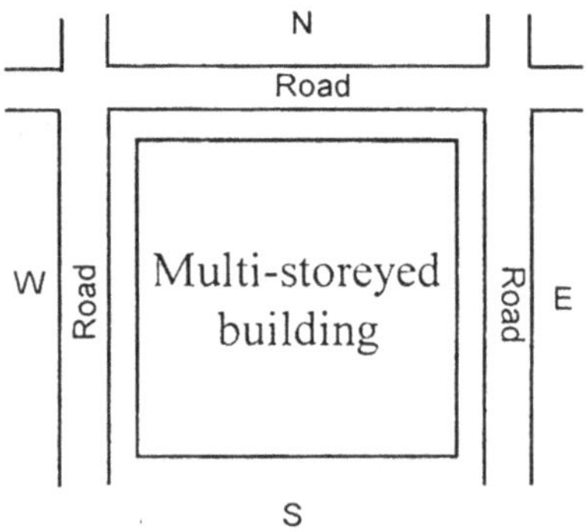

Multi-storeyed bldg with three side roads

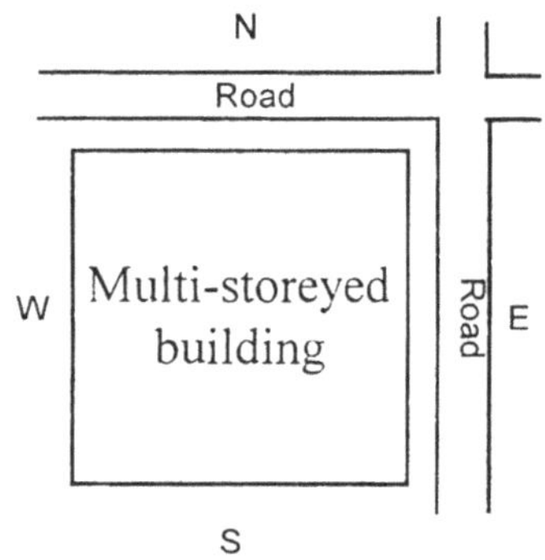

Multi-storeyed bldg auspicious for health & prosperity

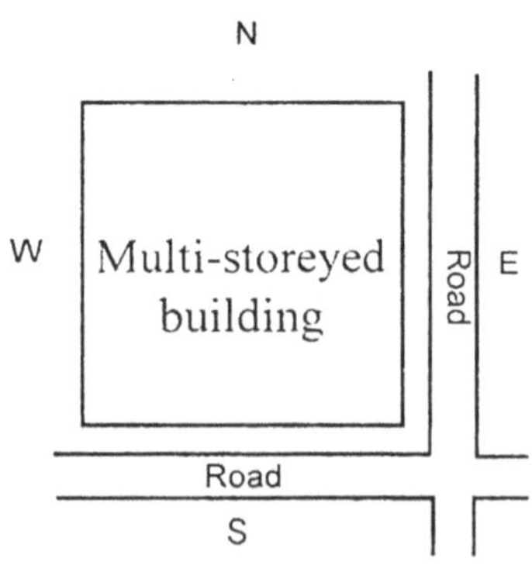

Multi-storeyed building auspicious exclusively to ladies related business

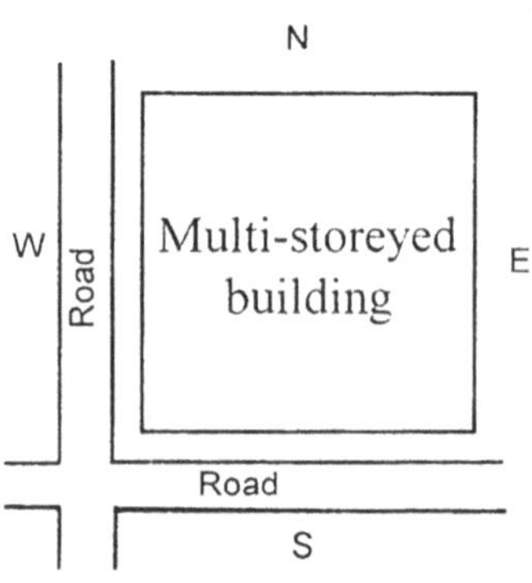

Multi-storeyed building auspicious for businessmen

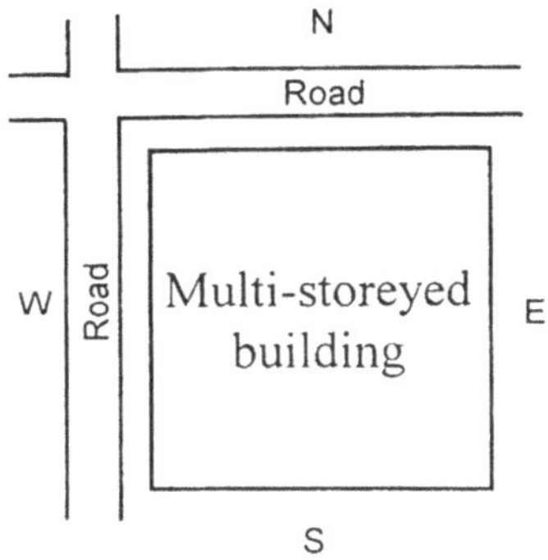

Auspicious for prosperity and fame

- Plot on the squares are always cut or rounded. If the plot of a multi-storeyed building is cut or rounded at south-east, south-west or north-west, there is no harm but if the plot is

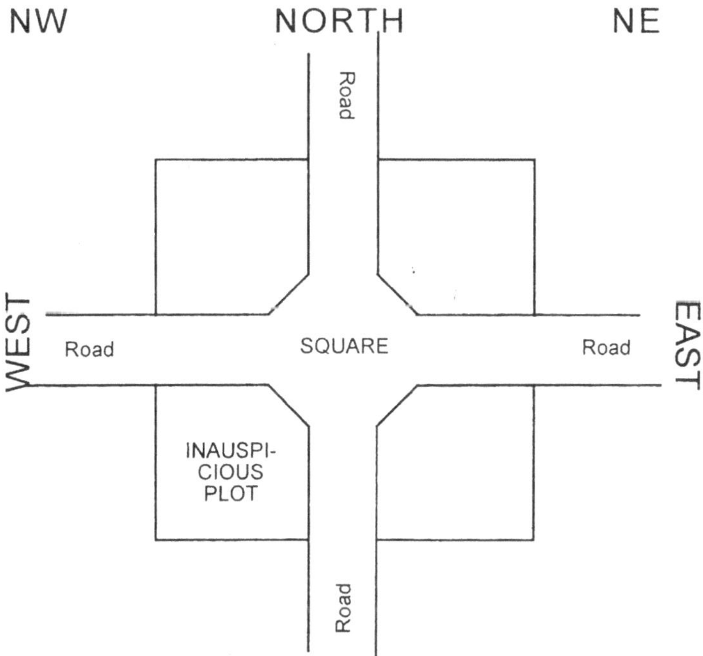

Three auspicious and one inauspicious plot on a square

cut at north-east it is inauspicious. One should not purchase a flat in such a building.

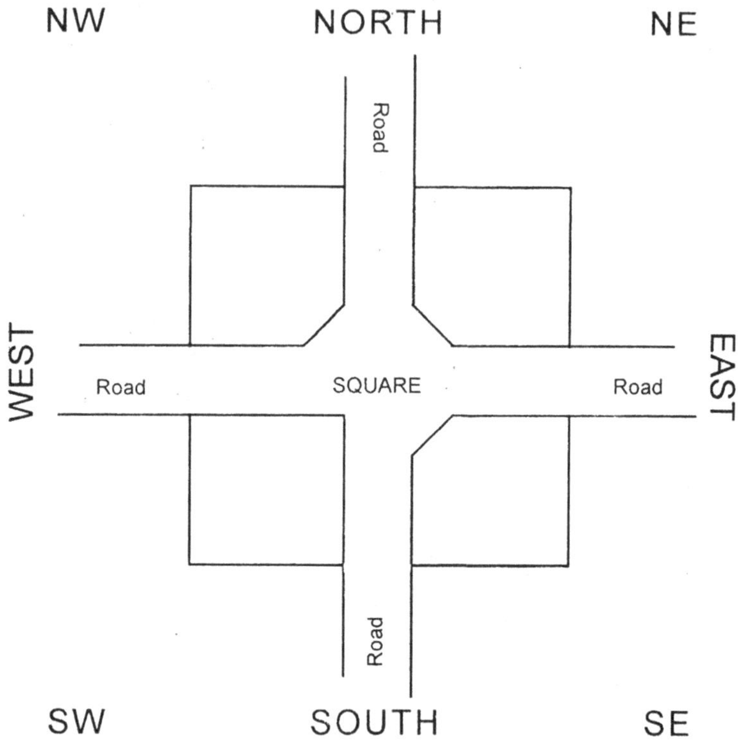

All four auspicious plots on a Square

- In cities most of the colonies, planned by development authorities or town development trusts have plots with adjoining main gates. Out of these mostly only on one plot a building can be constructed as per the Vaastu, in which the residents are happy. Whereas on the other plots construction cannot be done as per Vaastu, sometimes both such plots are not Vaastu favourable. Residents of such buildings are always unhappy. Hence flat in a multi-storeyed building on Vaastu defective plot should never be purchased.

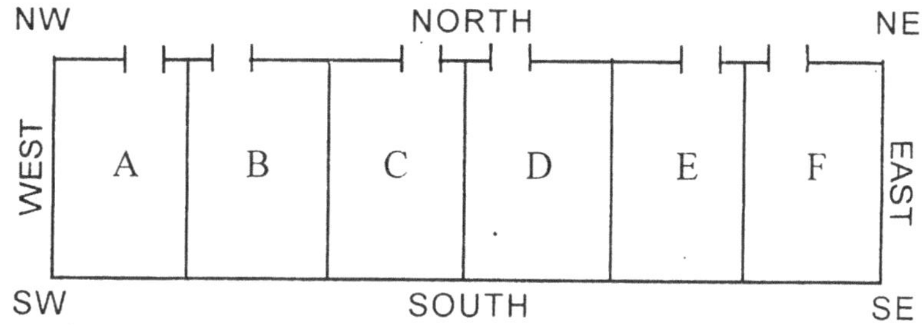

A,C & E are as per Vaastu and B,D & F are against Vaastu

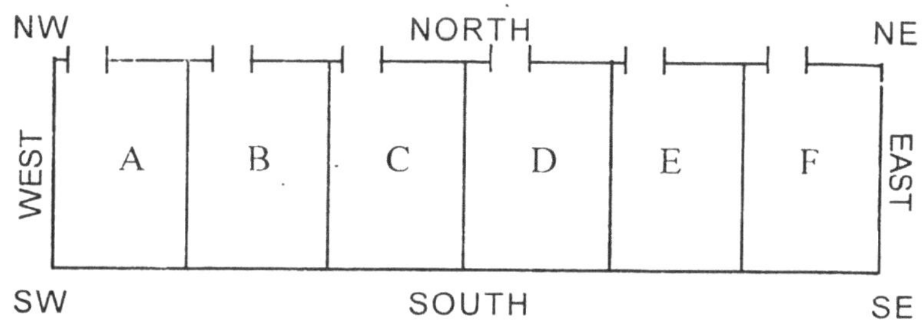

All the plots are against Vaastu

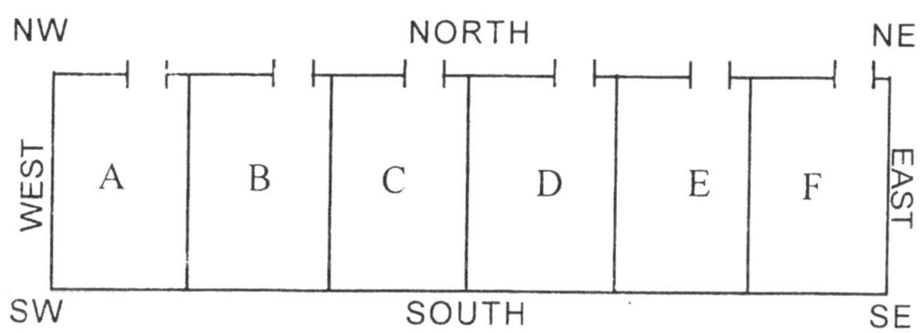

All the plots are as per Vaastu

COMPONUD WALL OF A MULTI-STOREYED BUILDING

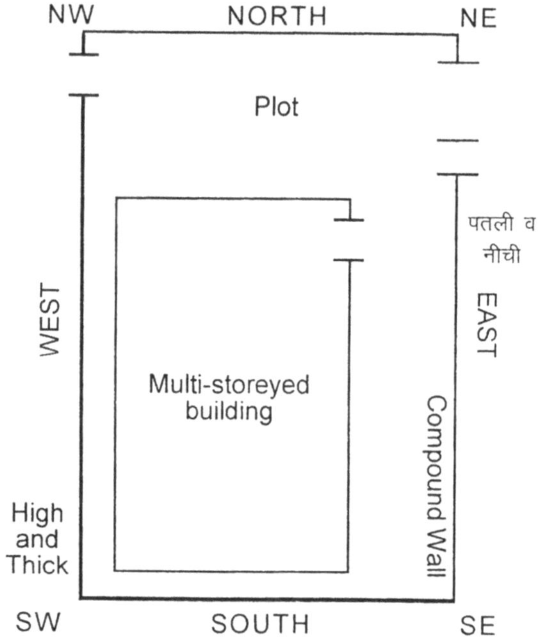

Ideal Compound Wall

It is very important to pay attention to the following things while constructing the compound wall.

- The compound wall should possess two gates, one main gate at front and other at the backside. Main entrance gate, in the front, should always be big. Back door should be smaller than the main gate. Main gate should be beautiful and grand. Such a main gate yields every happiness and prosperity.
- Main gate can be used for vehicles, while a small wicket

gate in it could be used for going on foot.

- Height of the compound wall should not be less than the two-third of the height of main gate.
- High and thick compound wall in the south-west direction is auspicious for health and wealth.
- The compound wall should be lowest in the north-east and highest in the south-west zone.
- While constructing the compound wall some space should be left in the east and north directions for the morning sun rays to enter the courtyard.
- South and west directions of the building can be used as compound wall.
- Underground car parking in the basement of a multi-storeyed building should be in the north, northeast or east direction. It creates lots of troubles for the residents if situated in the south, west or southwest direction.
- Nowadays multi-storeyed buildings have parking on the ground floor and the whole building is constructed on columns. Due to this there is a free flow of energy on the ground floor. One should not purchase a flat on the first floor of such a building, as the residents of the first floor do not have stability in life. Flats on any other floor can be purchased in such a building.
- Do not purchase a flat in a multi-storeyed building where base of the lift is prepared by digging a hole in the central, south, south-west or west. Residents of such a building lose health and money.
- Electric room or generator room of the building should be in the south-east direction.
- Overhead water tank of a multi-storeyed building should be in north-west, west or south-west direction. It should never be in the north-east direction.

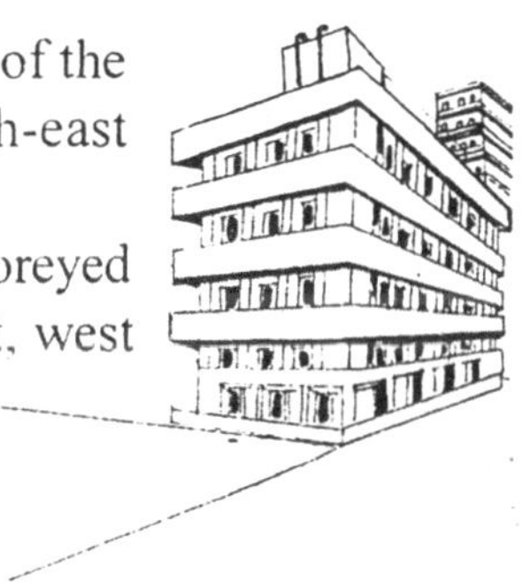

- While purchasing a flat on the top floor of a multi-storeyed building, make sure that overhead water tank is not directly above your flat. Residents of such a flat are under tremendous mental pressure. Many times they suffer from depression too.
- Staircase of the multi-storeyed building should never be in the north-east direction. It's auspicious if in the south or west and clockwise. Do not purchase a flat opposite to the staircase.
- Entrance of the flat should be hurdle free. It is auspicious.
- Vaastu defects are fully effective on the ground floor residents of a multi-storeyed building. It decreases as the floors increase. It is not auspicious to live on the top floor of a multi-storeyed building.

- Purchase a flat, which is airy, open and has morning sun rays. To get maximum benefit of the vital energy of the sunlight the balconies of the flat should be in the north, north-east and east direction.

- Small plants should be planted in the north, north-east and east so as not to obstruct the morning sun rays with vital energy. Big trees must be planted in south, south-east and west direction to protect from harmful heat and negative sun rays of the sun of afternoon.
- The kitchen of the flat is the best in the sout-heast. If its not possible then its better to construct kitchen in the northwest. Kitchen in any other direction is not recommended.
- The hearth of the kitchen should be arranged in the south east direction hence the kitchen platform should be prepared in the east direction. This will facilitate the opening of the hearth in the west direction and the food will be prepared facing east.
- In no circumstance the kitchen should be in the north-east direction of the flat. If the hearth is placed in the north-east direction then the flat owner becomes poor.

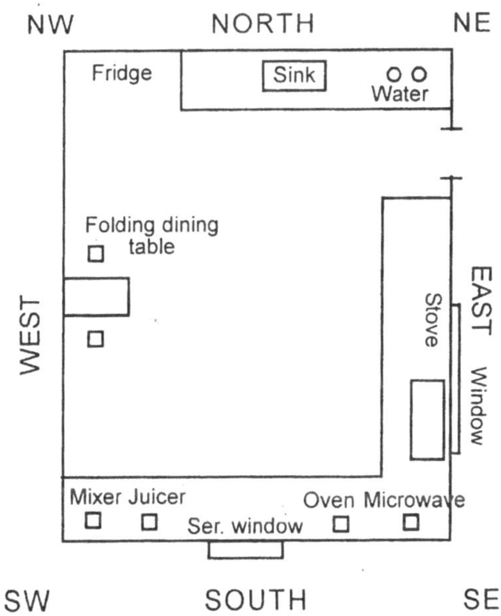

Model modern kitchen

- As per Vaastu and Feng Shui both, the water is precious. That's why leakage of tap water is supposed to be inauspicious. The leakage causes flow of money out of the home. Hence leaking taps should be taken care of immediately.

- As per Feng Shui it is auspicious to keep a painting, photograph or idol of pair of love birds of Manderian duck pair, which is symbol of romance, in the right side opposite to the entrance of the bedroom. This creates marriage of unmarried and increases love and affection between the married couple.

- Master bedroom and staircase in the north-east zone of the flat is inauspicious.
- Master bedroom should be in the south-west zone. Do not construct master bedroom in the north-east. Other bedroom can be constructed in south, west, north or east.

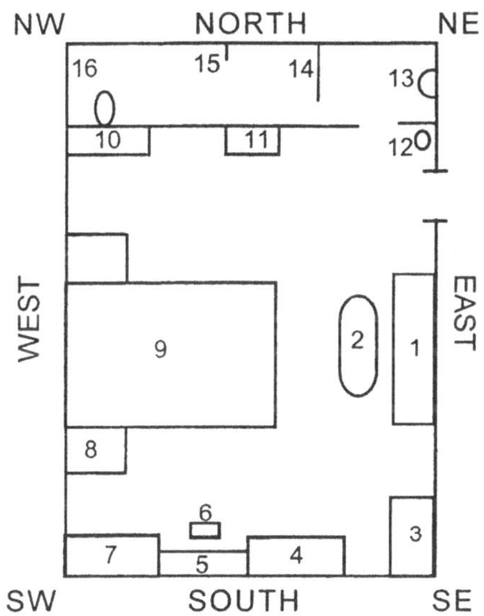

BEDROOM

1.	Sofa	9.	Bed
2.	Coffee Table	10.	Showcase/Almirah,
3.	T.V./ Computer	11.	Cooler/Fridge
4.	Almirah for wife	12.	Drinking Water
5.	Dressing Table	13.	Washbasin
6.	Stool	14.	Curtain/ Door
7.	Almirah for Husband	15.	Shower
8.	Bedside Table	16.	Commode

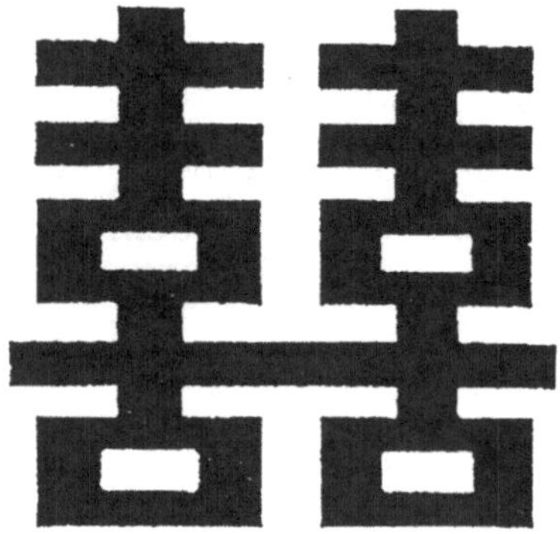

Double Happiness Symbol

- The red coloured 'double happiness symbol' is very effective as per Feng Shui. Wherever it is kept that region is filled with energy. It's auspicious to put it on the wall opposite to the entrance of the bedroom.
- Guest room and the bedroom of the girls of the family should be in the north-west direction of the flat. The bedroom of the girls should never be constructed in the south-west direction.

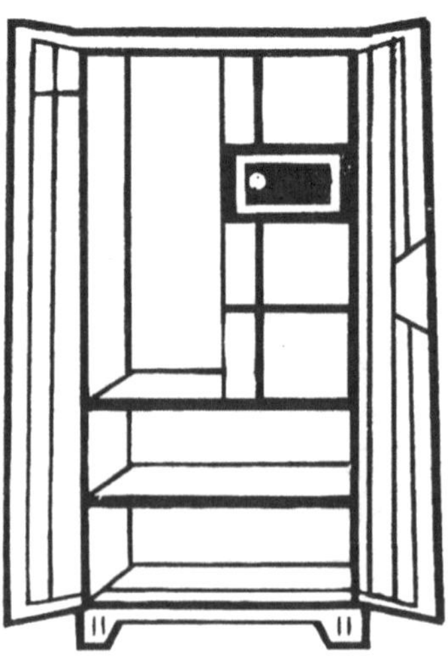

- Safe in which the cash and jewellery should be kept with the wall in south or west direction. Thus the doors will open in the north or east direction. Never keep safe in the north-east direction it yields financial loss.
- If possible then construct drawing room in the north-east zone and the dining room in the west direction of the flat. Drawing room and dining room should never be constructed in the south-west zone.

- A crystal ball should be put in the right corner of the wall opposite to the entrance of the drawing room. It fills the corner with energy. This also keeps healthy and warm relations with friends and relatives. It also adds to your fame.

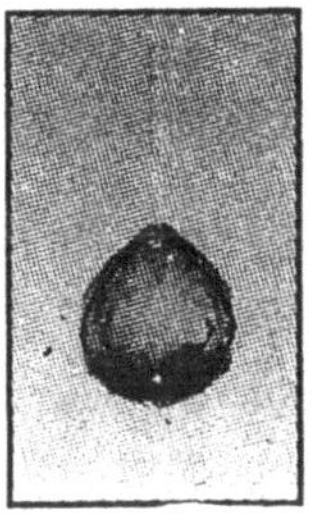

- Never put any painting, photograph or idol showing violent beasts, sad scenes, crying, sun set, ship and stagnant water on the walls of the rooms. This brings bad luck, tension and disappointment in the life.

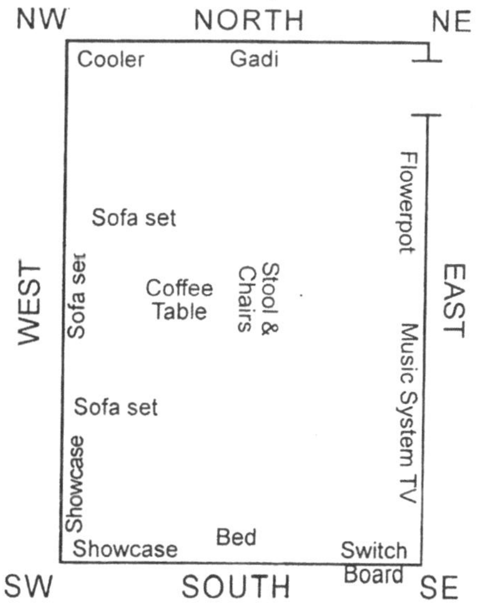

Drawing room as per Vaastu

- Fortune is strengthened if some gold fishes are kept in a fish pot, in the flat. There must be eight red and no black fishes. Drawing room is the best place to keep aquarium. It should be kept to the right hand while entering.
- Study room of the children should be in north-east zone or west direction. If children face north or east, while studying then they get best results with less work.

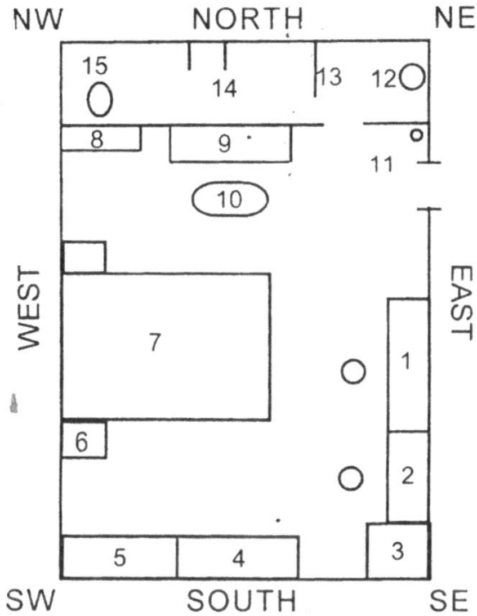

Model study-cum-bedroom for students

1. Study Table	2. Computer
3. T.V.	4. Rack for the books
5. Almirah	6. Bedside Table
7. Bed	8. Dressing Table
9. Sofa	10. Tea Table
11. Drinking Water	12. Washbasin
13. Curtain	14. Tap
15. Commode	

- Toilet in the north-east zone of the flat flushes money and brings ill fame. Toilets are decorated these days. This is opposite to Vaastu, because if toilet is decorated much positive energy gathered in the home is flushed.

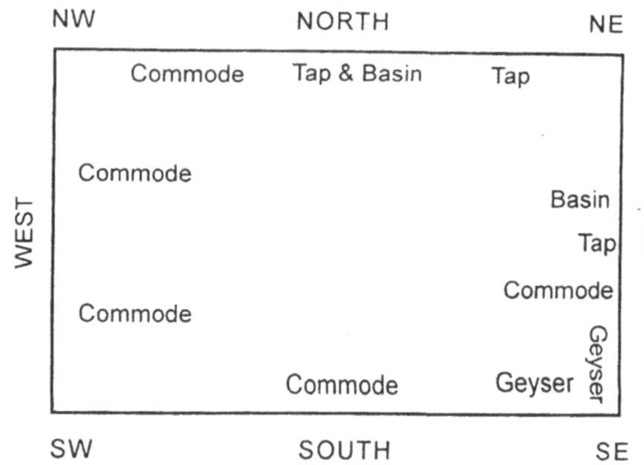

Toilet/Bathroom

- Septic tank of the multi-storeyed building should be in north-east or south-west zone.

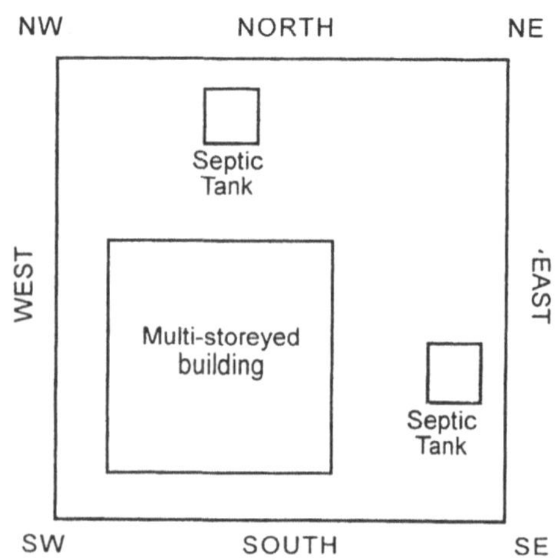

- Cactus, Bonsai, dry flowers, heads of beasts, skin etc. produce negative energy hence do not kept them in the flat.

- A beautiful nameplate, made up of wood, plastic or any metal should be put outside the flat at a visible place. It brings fame.

- Staircase in front of the entrance of the flat is not auspicious. This defect could be removed by hanging 5 rod wind chime outside the main gate.

- As per the Feng Shui end of an ascending staircase in front of the main entrance of the flat is inauspicious. It could be removed by putting Pa-kua with a concave Mirror.

- As per Feng Shui origin of an ascending staircase in front of the main door of the flat is inauspicious. To eradicate the effect of this the door frame should be lifted by two inches.

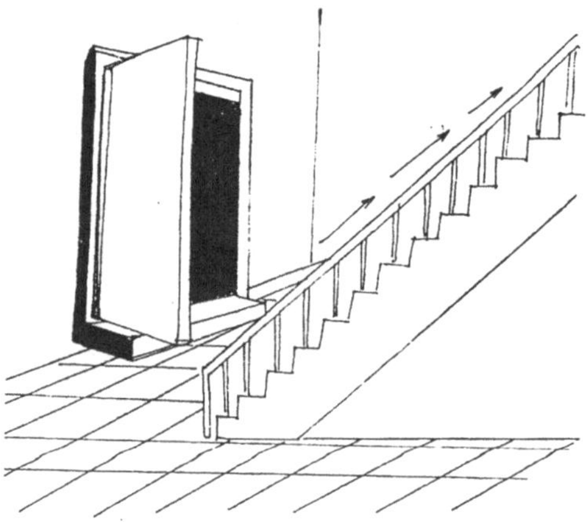

- Earthen flowerpots should be placed to either side of the main entrance of the flat. These make the energy entering the house more positive which helps in the increase of the fame. Make sure that the plants in the earthen flowerpots should be of broad leaves and never with thorny or pointed leaves.

- Windows on either side of the main entrance of the flat are inauspicious. It is believed that with the air fortune also flows out through these windows. In such a condition plants with round leaves in earthen flowerpots should be kept on the windows.

Mirror is very significant in the Feng Shui. An octagonal shape is considered very sacred in the China. Octagonal Pa Kua, having a small mirror. This small mirror centers the energy and becomes very powerful. Placed inside or outside of the window or main entrance, Pa Kua mirror reflects back the inauspicious energy like the poisonous arrows.

- Auspicious symbols as per our faith such as *Swastika*, *Om*, *Trishool* and Cross etc. should be placed on the main entrance of the flat. This gives fortune, fame and prosperity.

- A call bell should always be placed on the main entrance of the flat. This call bell should always be switched on. The positive energy gathered on the main door is destroyed, if somebody calls or knocks at the door.

- A bouquet of flowers or small bells should be kept outside the main entrance of the flat. This invites the fortune.
- Automatic opening and closing of the main door of the flat is inauspicious. The hinges should be lubricated if the door squeaks.

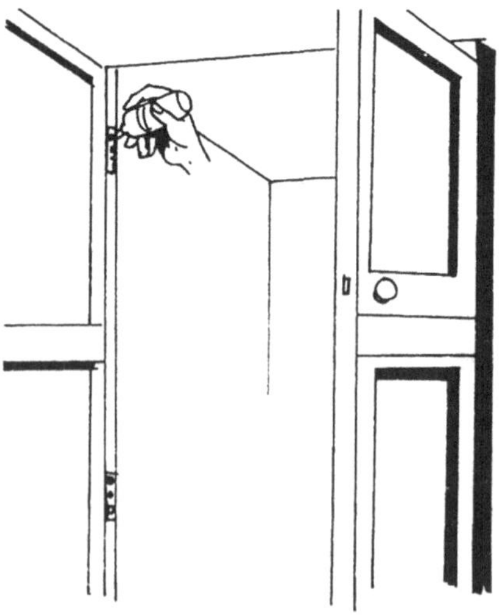

- The main door of the flat should open fully without noise, so as to give way to maximum positive energy in the flat.

- It is inauspicious to keep footwears in front of the main entrance of the flat. This obstructs the entry of the positive energy.
- It is inauspicious to hang something behind the main entrance of the flat. This interferes with the fame.

- The main entrance and its surroundings must be kept clean so as to make way to the positive energy.

- The colour and polish etc. of the main entrance of the flat should always be maintained to invite the positive energy. Broken, dirty and rusted main door produces negative energy and is fatal to the fame.
- A mirror on the main entrance reflects back the entering positive energy and good opportunities are also returned back.

- The horseshoe is considered auspicious in many countries. It accumulates a lot of energy due to continuous running while fixed to the horse leg. It is termed auspicious when put on doorframe. It should be put as the reverse of the English alphabet "U".

- Ringing of the small temple bell, every morning and evening in the flat, produces vibrations which destroy the negative energy.

- It is compulsory to keep the house clean in daily life. A dirty house poses health problems to the residents. A lot of rubbish is produced in the houses nowadays due to available packaged daily items. This rubbish should never be put in the north-east and in front of the main entrance of the house. A dustbin can be put in any other place, barring these two, in the house.
- Opening of a toilet door in front of the flat or either to the right or left, is inauspicious as it scatters negative energy in the house. If it is so this door should be closed and opened in the opposite direction.

- Wiping of the flat with salt water destroys negative energy and increases positive energy.

- It is auspicious to keep some dry-sea salt in the toilet of the flat. It absorbs the negative energy of its surroundings. When moist this salt should be replaced.

- Any non-functioning clock, TV and radio etc. should not be kept in the flat. These obstruct the progress of the life.

- Unuseful material, scrap, broken furniture and spider web etc. increase negative energy in the flat and obstruct the positive one.
- Do not purchase a flat in a multi-storeyed building situated near big hospital, crematorium, butchery and police station. Due to gloomy atmosphere, the negative energy is in plenty at such places which affects the mental condition of the residents.

OFFICE – VAASTU AND FENG SHUI

Commercial activities are carried out in an office nowadays. A cut-throat competition in the business results in struggle of an entrepreneur for success. In such difficult times the construction and decoration of the office as per the Vaastushastra and Feng Shui principles is advantageous.

The efficiency of the employees of an office not as per the Vaastu principles is affected a lot. They are irritable and there are disputes in between the officers and the employees. There are a lot of other problems in the office too. On the contrary construction of the office as per the Vaastu principles makes the atmosphere cheerful, all the employees and officers are tension free. their working efficiency is good. They work together happily and get promotion according to their ability from time to time.

Purchase a Vaastu suitable place for the office and decorate it as below:

- A beautiful signboard made up of wood, plastic or metal should be placed outside the office in such a way that it is visible to everyone passing by it increases the fame of the office.

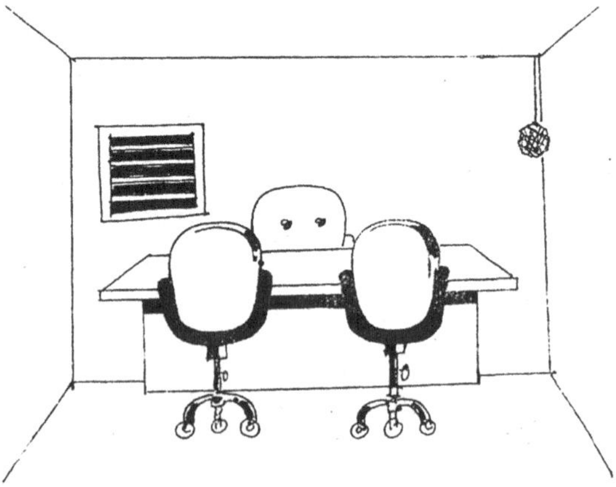

- As per Feng Shui a crystal ball inside the office on right hand corner of the wall opposite to the door makes that corner full of energy. This makes the relationship of the visitors and the employees happy.

- The room of the chief of the office should be in the south-west zone. The shape of this room should be square or rectangular. It should never be uneven.

- The chief should sit in south or west facing north or east.
- The room of the chief should never be constructed in a narrow lane or a basement.
- The rooms of all the subordinates of the chief should be in the south or west.
- The account department should be in the south or the east and the accountant should sit facing north.
- The room of the cashier should be in such a position, in the north, that he may see anybody entering the office through the main entrance.
- The safe (cash box) of the office should be kept along with the south facing the north direction.
- The reception of the office should be constructed in the north-east zone, north or east. The receptionist should sit facing north or east. The visitors should face west or south while entering the office.

- It is auspicious to construct the room for the field staff i.e. sales man etc. in the north-west zone.
- The post and dispatch department of the office should be in the south or the west direction.

- The conference hall should be in the north or west of the north-west zone of the office. Here an oval table and 15-20 chairs should be kept for meeting.
- The chair of the chief of the office should be kept in such a way that he should face east or north in such a way that he could watch anybody entering the room.
- If a place is needed in the conference room to keep the files then it must be in the south-west zone of the office. It could also be constructed in the south or west if needed.
- It is good to have that office table in square or rectangular shape. Octagonal or square shaped tables are auspicious as per Feng Shui also.
- The office table should be kept in such a way that every on-goer is watched properly.

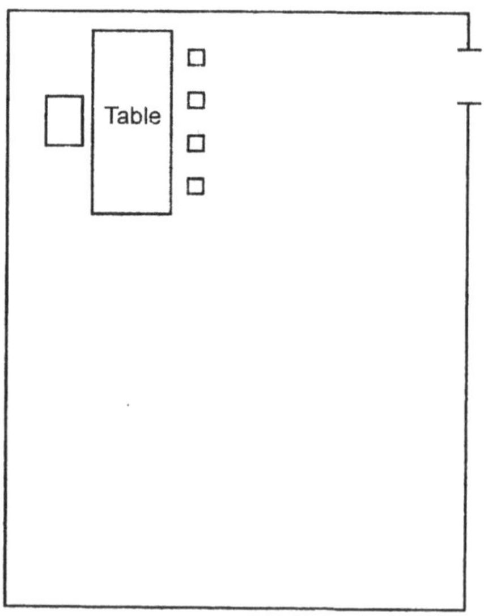

Table kept opposite to the office door

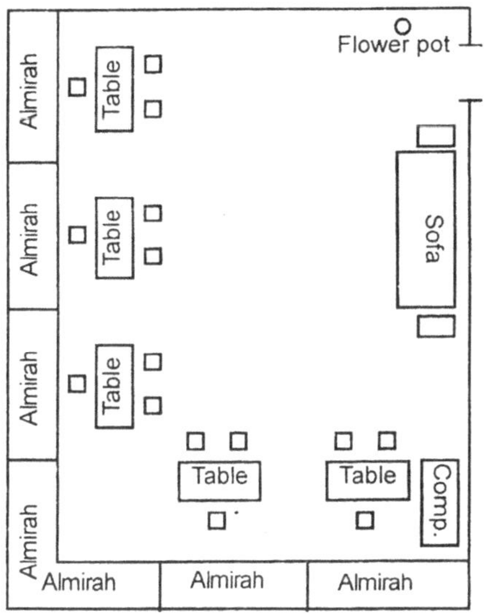

Ideal sitting arrangement in the office

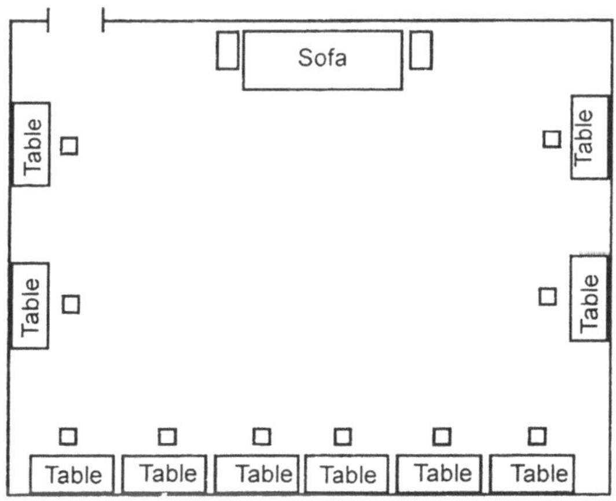

Wrong sitting arrangement in the office

- Do not keep table opposite to the office door. This increases mental tension of the employee, which affects his working efficiency.

- The place where the employees sit should not be below any beam or loft, because this increases their mental tension which in turn affects their efficiency. If due to some problem it is necessary to sit below a beam or loft than this defect should be removed by hanging two flutes in a red ribbon at 45^0.

- The sitting arrangement in the office should be in such a manner that the employees should face east or North direction while working. No employee should keep his back towards the main door.

- The size of the table should be proportionate to the size of room. If the table is of big size then the employee feels fatigue and if the table is small then he is under-confidant.

- Telephone and fax on the table should be kept in the southeast zone of the table. Similarly the glass of water should be kept in the northeast zone of the table.

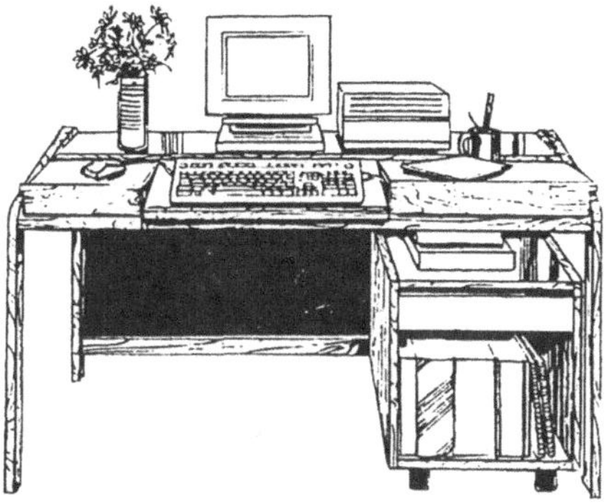

- The computer should be kept in the southeast zone of any room in the office.
- File cabinets of every room of the office should be in the south or the west of the room.

- The recreation room of the office staff should be in the north-west zone of the office.
- The colour of the walls and the curtains of the office should be light. It keeps the mind of the workers of office cool. The dark colours produce aggression.
- The flowerpot in the office should be kept in the east or the north-east zone of any room of the office.

- Do not put photographs, paintings or idols of violent. sad or crying beasts or birds, sunset and drowning ship on the walls or the curtains of any room of the office. These create disappointment in life of the employees and affect their efficiency.
- Water is treated as wealth in Vaastu and Feng Shui both. Leaking of water from any tap in the office is inauspicious. The money flows out like water in such condition. These should be repaired at once.
- The drinking water arrangement in the office like water cooler etc. can be kept in the north or east direction. Kitchen or pantry should be in the south-east zone of the office.
- Door of a toilet opposite or on either side of the main door of the office is inauspicious. It spreads negative energy in the whole house. In such a case the door of the toilet should be closed and constructed in another direction.
- No employee should sit facing the door of the toilet in the office.
- Toilet attached to the room of the officers should never be in the north-east zone of the office.
- While cleaning the office, the floor should be wiped with salt water. It destroys the negative energy and increases the positive energy.
- It is auspicious to put some dry sea salt in a glass bowl in the toilet of the office. It absorbs the whole negative energy present in the toilet. When it is wet due to moisture, it should be replaced.
- There should not be any out of order clock, telephone, fax, photocopy machine etc. as these things create hindrances in the lives of the employees.
- Do not purchase office in a building situated near, big hospital, crematorium, butchery and police station. Due to gloomy atmosphere the negative energy is in plenty at such places, which affects the mental health of the employees. If there is a public road in between then this bad effect is removed.

PENTHOUSE AND VAASTU

During my 17th journey to the UAE, Mr. Ashok Shetty in Sharjah invited me for dinner. He had a penthouse on the terrace of a multi-storeyed building in Sharjah. The decoration of the penthouse was grand and showed good taste of my host. Mr. Shetty told me in the course of the conversation that he was a general trader. With the blessings of the fortune he had some good opportunities in business. He had shifted to that grand penthouse only one year back but was perturbed due to continuous losses incurred in the business. He was losing money continuously just after he shifted in this penthouse. He was unable to understand the reason thereof, as the working style was the same.

Being a Vaastu consultant I always wear a compass just like a wristwatch. I have a habit to give a look to my compass while entering in a new house. I had already had an idea about the problems of Mr. Shetty as my habitual look at the compass had suggested to me that the penthouse was not constructed as per the Vaastu principles.

Rooms in the penthouse were constructed in the north, east and north-east zone. The south-west was opening where he had a kitchen garden. In the centre there were table tennis and snooker tables. The master bedroom was in the north-east with an attached toilet. All these were contradictory to the Vaastu principles.

No foreigner can purchase any property in the UAE. All the foreigners reside on rent. It is almost impossible to make any changes in a multi-storeyed building. I, therefore, suggested him to leave that penthouse and shift in any other house which should be as per the Vaastu principles.

He took a year to make up his mind to abide by my suggestion and shifted in a flat constructed as per the Vaastu principles.

After a few days all the conditions of the business of Mr. Shetty improved and now his business is running smoothly. Due to this he has invested heavily in the real estate in Mangalore city of south India.

To construct a penthouse on the terrace of a building or multi-storeyed building is the latest trend among the rich now a day. Newly married couples or the persons fond of penthouse decorate them beautifully and live therein.

If Vaastu principles are formed while purchasing or constructing a penthouse, enjoyment of its residents is increased many fold and others are impressed too:

- Rooms of the penthouse on the terrace should be constructed in square or rectangular shape in the south and west direction, leaving maximum space in the north and east directions. Care should be taken to construct the rooms with right angles. A grand and happy life could be lived in such a Vaastu supported penthouse.
- Depressed, cut and round north, east directions and north-east zone of the penthouse are inauspicious. On the contrary if all these directions are big in size then it is auspicious.
- The entrance and the exit of the penthouse should be as per the markings in the figure. If the entrance is kept on the place marked 'X', it creates a lot of troubles in the life.
- A toilet in the north-east of the penthouse flushes the money and creates financial problems. To decorate the toilets is the latest fashion. It is against the principles of Vaastu, because it flushes the positive energy collected in the house.

- The swimming pool in the penthouse should be constructed in the north or east direction.
- Water is considered as wealth in Vaastu. Hence any leakage in the kitchen, bathroom or anywhere in the penthouse should be fixed immediately as this flushes money out of the penthouse like water.
- The temple should be in the north-east zone of the penthouse for good health. This facilitates the benefit of the vital morning Sun rays.
- If interested in the thinking, mediation and yoga, their place should be in the east or north-east zone. Library could be constructed in the west direction, if interested in studies.
- Health club, massage room and steam bath etc. should be constructed in the north-west zone of the penthouse. Indoor games like table tennis and snooker table etc. for the recreation of the guests could be around these facilities.
- The rooms of a penthouse should be in the south and west directions or south-west zone. More windows should be in the east and north of the rooms. Beds in the rooms should be kept in such a way that legs should be in the north and head in the south direction while sleeping.
- Never construct a penthouse in a place from where the high-tension wires of electricity supply pass. The electro-magnetic rays emitted from them affect the health of the residents.
- Meter of the electricity supply, transformer, generator and other electrical appliances should be in the south-east zone.
- Barbecue for the parties in the house should be done in the south-east zone.
- Overhead water tank could be constructed anywhere from west of the north-west to the south of the south-west zone.

- The colours of the inner and outer walls of the penthouse should be sober and light. This creates peace in the mind. The dark colours initially look attractive but later on make the residents violent in their nature.
- A garden could be created in the north and east direction of the penthouse. A greenhouse, lower in height than that of the main building, could be prepared in the south-east or north-west zone.
- To plant cactus, plants with pointed leaves and plants emitting milk is inauspicious. The milk emitted by most of the plants is poisonous. It troubles with vision when in contact with eyes and sometimes makes a person blind.
- Never keep plants inside the penthouse in the night as these exhale carbon dioxide, which affects the health of those sleeping there.
- Never put a climber in the garden of the penthouse. These produce problems.
- There should be ample light near the entrance of the penthouse. Some beautiful earthen flowerpots should also be kept on either side of the entrance. These make the positive energy entering the penthouse more positive and help in making you prosperous. But these plants in the earthen flowerpots should be of broad leaves and not of the pointed leaves.
- Putting the symbols as per ones faith, e.g. *Swastika*, *Om*, *Trishul* and Cross etc. on the main entrance of the penthouse increases fortune.
- Cactus, dry flowers, heads of the beasts and their skin should not be kept in the penthouse as these all increase negative energy.
- Bonsai plants should never be kept in the penthouse. They may look good but they are the symbols of hurdles in the development and prosperity of the normal life.
- There should not be any out of order viz. clock, TV, tape

recorder and radio etc. in the penthouse. These obstruct progress in the life.

- Do not purchase the penthouse of an unsuccessful and unfortunate person, because there must be certain Vaastu defect there, which could disturb you and make your life miserable. Such a penthouse can only be used after the removal of its Vaastu defect.

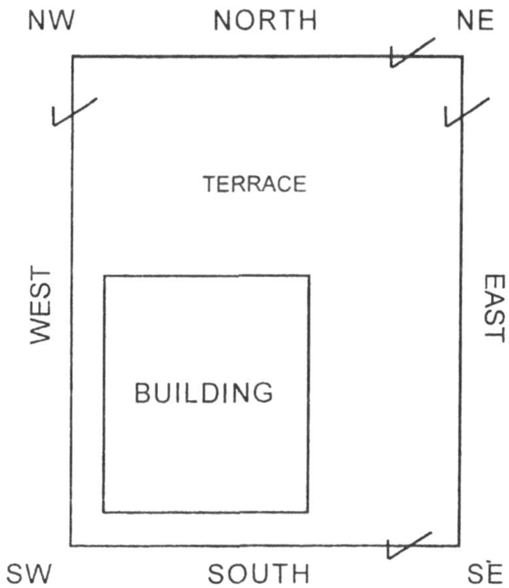

TENANT AND VAASTU

In this era of costly life people keep on searching for different sources of income. Income from tenancy is also one of them. The owner gives a part of his house on rent for this income.

Recently, Mr. Goyal of Delhi rented out a part of his house for certain extra income to make his life more comfortable. But on the contrary, he found that in spite of getting a comfortable life, he was getting troubles and the life was much tougher now. His money was being wasted instead of accumulation. Then arguments with his tenant started without any apparent reasons. Matters were dragged up to the courts too. During this he came in my contact and informed me about his problems. I could make out the main reason behind all his problems on my visit to his house. Unknowingly some Vaastu principles were violated while he rented his house. He had rented out the north and north-east zone of his house. The entrance of the tenant in the house was in the east of the south-east and that of Mr. Goyal was in the south-east after he rented his house.

As per the Vaastu principle cut, depressed or small north-east zone of any place is inauspicious and entrance of any place from the south-east zone produces quarrels.

On my suggestion, Mr. Goyal had truce with his tenant and he vacated his house. He then turned the house in its old condition. This change gradually made his life happy again.

There is a belief among the common people that it is inauspicious to rent out a part of the house in which the owner is living. This is completely wrong; a part of the house could be rented if the Vaastu principles are abided while renting a part of the house. The landlord and tenant could live together with love, affection and dignity. In addition, the landlord will get an additional income.

The north, east and north-east zone of the house should never be rented out. The landlord should keep it for self-use. Only south, west and south-west zone of the house should be rented out. East of the north-east zone, south and west part should be rented out if there is a road in the east of the house. The landlord should live in the east and north-east zone.

North of the north-west zone, south of the south-east zone, south and west part of the house should be rented out if there is a road in the north of the house. The landlord should live in the north, east and north-east zone.

If a tenant vacates and south-west part of the house is unused then it creates a lot of problems. In such a condition the landlord should himself use this unused part until a new tenant comes, because used north-east direction and unused south-west direction produce incredible losses.

Vaastu defects affect both the tenant and the landlord, equally. Therefore, if the principles of Vaastu are not followed while the house is rented out, then the consequences are to be faced by both the tenant and the landlord.

It is best to construct the house in such a way that when it is rented out, at the time of need the division is as per the Vaastu principles. This division should be such that the tenant and the landlord both should possess the part of the house in square or rectangular shape. No part or direction of the house should be cut or protruded. The entrances of both should be as per Vaastu.

BANK AND VAASTU

In the modern times the utility of the banks, for business transactions, loans for business, safe investment of saved money, lockers for the precious things and loans for house and vehicles, is increasing day by day. The banks are opening their branches from metro cities to small towns. They provide many facilities to attract their customers.

It has been observed that some branches of a bank do very good business whereas others run into heavy losses since their beginning. Some banks have been cheated and in some banks the customers have been looted and cheated.

In my own town the branch of a bank is running into losses since many years. There is lack of coordination between the officers and the employees, customers are not treated well and many other problems are also there. Significant Vaastu defect in the plot and the building of that bank is the main reason behind all these problems. The north-east zone of that bank is depressed. Strongroom of the bank is in basement in the centre of the building. The main entrance of the bank is in the south of the southwest zone and other entrance is in the south of the south-east zone.

If the basic principles of Vaastu are followed while opening a bank branch, then there is good coordination between officers and employees. Customers are happy. Such branches run successfully and earn good profit:

- Bank branch should be opened in such a building, which is constructed at right angle on a right-angled plot only. Do not open branch in building constructed on an irregular plot.
- If the bank building is constructed on a big plot then more

open space should be left in the east and north than in the south and west.

- It is inauspicious to have cut, depressed and round north, east and north-east zone of the plot or building of a bank. Banks on such a plot are always in loss. Opposite to this all these directions, big plots are auspicious.
- Open the branch in such a building where the under ground water source is in the north, east and north-east zone. If the water source is in other direction than these, do not open the branch there. Overhead water tank should be in the south or west direction.
- Floor level of the branch should be even or lower in the north, east and north-east zone and south, west and south-west zone should be higher.
- The main entrance and exit of the bank should be in the east of the north-east zone, south of the south-east, west of the north-west or north of the north-east zone. They should never be in the east of the south-east, south or west of the south-west or north of the north-west zone.
- Electric meter, generator and other electric appliances should be kept in the south-east zone.
- The colour of the curtains, walls and furniture should be of light yellow or cream colour. Yellow is the colour of the god of money 'Kuber'.
- The cabin of the bank manager should be in the south or the south-west zone. The placement of the furniture should be such that the manager should sit facing north or east.
- The filing cabinet in the room of the manager should be in the south or west direction.
- The sitting arrangement of the bank staff should be such that there should not be any overhead loft or beam. If there is a beam or loft on the head of an employee, then he does not feel good, remain in tension all the time and cannot do work assigned to him properly.

- The sitting arrangement of the employees should be such that they should face north or east while working on their seats.
- The computers of the officers and employees should be placed in the south-east zone of the table.
- Cash counters of the bank should be made in the north in such a way that the cashier may sit facing east or north direction.
- Cash counters of the bank should be placed in the south direction in such a way that their drawers open in the north direction.
- The receipt counter of the cash deposit should be in the central part of the north direction. Cash payment counter should be in the west side of the north direction.
- Loan disbursement counters should be in the north-east zone.
- Waiting room for the customers in the bank should be prepared in the north-west zone. Empty vouchers to be used by the customers, should be placed in the north of the waiting room. The electronic token machine should be placed in the south-east zone of the waiting room.
- The strongroom of the bank should be in the south direction. The lockers in the strongroom should be kept along with the south or west walls in such a way that they open in the north or east direction. The lockers should not be kept in front of the entrance.
- If the strongroom is to be constructed in the basement, then the basement should be in north, north-east zone or east direction.
- The lockers of the bank should not be kept under any loft or beam. The ventilatiors of the locker room should be in the east direction only.
- The room where all the old documents, such as registers, files, voucher and other stationery is kept should be constructed in the south-west zone.

- The entrances of the cabin of the manager, cabins of all other officers and strongroom of the bank etc. should be in the east of the north-east zone, south of the south-east zone, west of the south-west zone and north of the north-east zone, at one place only.
- The enquiry counter in the bank should be in the east direction.
- The meeting hall and recreation hall of the staff should be in the west direction.
- The canteen of the bank should be in the south-east zone.
- Arrangement of the drinking water and the water cooler should be in the north or east direction.
- Urinals and the toilets should be prepared in the west or north-west zone.
- The staircase to go upstairs in the bank should be constructed in south, west or south-west zone, in such a way that there is a right hand turn while going upstairs.
- Parking for the staff and customers should be in the north or east direction.
- If there is an open space in the north-east zone of the bank then a small lawn should be prepared there. Similarly, in the open space of the south-west zone, big trees should be planted.

SHOPPING COMPLEX AND VAASTU

Eight years back Mr. Bhatia, a famous clock businessman of Dubai, wanted to open a new shop in Sharjah (UAE) for the expansion of his business. I was in Dubai those days. Mr. Bhatia contacted me and asked for help to select a Vaastu suitable shop in a newly constructed shopping complex in Sharjah. I accompanied him and saw the shopping complex, which was constructed in the "L" shape. It was grand and had many big shops. The rent of its smallest shop was almost equal to Rs. 1,500,000. This "L" shaped complex had its arms in the north and east directions and parking lot in the open space in south and west. All the shops of the complex had glass in the front and glass doors too. The shops of the east direction had their entrances in the west of the south-west zone and the shops of the north direction had their entrances in the south of the south-west. It was not possible to get the permission from Municipal Corporation of Sharjah to change the direction of the entrances. I advised Mr. Bhatia not to purchase a shop in this complex as it was constructed against the principles of Vaastu. It was not possible to run a business successfully in this complex. I did not see any possibility of success for the complex. Mr. Bhatia had confidence in my ability and followed my advice and did not purchase any shop in that complex. It is almost and years since then and that complex is sill vacate and ruined now. Many tenants came and then vacated the shops after loss.

In my hometown too, many shopping complexes have been built fully equipped with all the modern facilities. Many of these are in a sorry state due to lack of the customers, many are with incomplete construction. Some have complete buildings but no shutters, construction of some is held up due to orders of the court. All these incomplete complexes have some very significant Vaastu defects. For example, some of them have pit for lift in the south-west zone, well in the centre, a door with the basement in the south of the south-west zone, cut north-east zone, protruded south-west zone etc. A residential-cum-shopping complex of my town was a success from the beginning. Because the flats and the shops of this complex were sold out at once, many other complexes were started in different places of the town. People who had purchased flats and shops in that successful complex decorated their places and started living and doing business there. Now the builder expanded the complex in the open space in north, east and north-east zone. This expansion created many Vaastu defects in the good Vaastu of the complex. For example, a well situated in the east was filled, construction was done in the north, east and north-east zone. This reduced open space in the north, east and north-east zone in comparison to south, west and south-west zone. To go upstairs in the flat, a door was placed a few feet inside, this produced a cut in the east direction of the plot of the complex. A bore-well was dug in the south of the south-west zone. Due to these Vaastu defects an innocent girl died in a lift accident there. There have been many violent incidences in a restaurant of the complex, because the main entrance of the same is in the south of the south-west zone. The bore-well is also in front in the south direction. Similarly, the shops of the complexes, which were running successfully, now have started closing gradually. Office of a prestigious company was closed due to some disputes. Now some of the flat and shop owners want to sell their properties in the complex.

But now the customers are not interested and if somebody is interested the price offered is very low. Slowly a very successful complex is being ruined.

In Ujjain city a basement has been constructed, against the Vaastu principles, in a complex near Shaheed Park. The entrance of the basement is in the west of the south-west zone. The owner of the complex has been under loss while selling this complex. Some part of this complex is still unoccupied. There has been a murder on the gate of the basement recently.

It costs a lot to construct a commercial complex. The architects produce beautiful drawings. Thus constructed complex looks beautiful. But no matter how beautiful this may be, if the construction is not as per the Vaastu then the builder has to face a lot of troubles. The shops are not easily sold out. In general the builder runs into heavy losses. If some body, by mistake purchases a shop in such a Vaastu defected complex then he loses financially.

I have had opportunity to visit many cities of India. I have seen many complexes; most of them are a failure due to Vaastu defects. The builder as well the purchasers of such complexes are in loss. The shopping complexes, which are constructed as per the Vaastu principles, have brightness and movement of the customers' whole day. The customers as well as the businessmen both enjoy business in such shopping complexes, which are constructed as per Vaastu.

The builder and the businessmen of a shopping complex earn attractive profits and do their business smoothly, if the construction is done as per the following Vaastu principles:

- Select a plot which is right angled and is in the centre or at an easily accessible place of the city.
- The level of the plot, on which the shopping complex is to be constructed, should be plain or lower in the north, east and north-east zone and higher in the south, west and southwest zone.

Special : The builder should enter into an agreement with the buyer or any tenant that the latter would not create any underground water source except in the north, east and north-east zone.

- The underground water source a shopping complex, should only be in the north, east and north-east zone. This gives financial boom to the builder and shop owners both.
- The building of the shopping complex should be constructed in the south-west zone of the plot. The shops in it should be of right-angle and not any odd angle. More open space should be left in the north, east and north-east zone.
- More windows should be constructed in the north or east than in the south or west direction.
- The lofts in the shops of the complex should be in walls of the south or west direction.
- The staircase of the shopping complex should be in the south, west and south-west zone, with an ascending right turn.
- The lift should be kept in the south, west and south-west zone. Care should be taken not to create any pit in these directions, while placing the lift, as this produces a Vaastu defect, which becomes cause for many problems. The lift should be placed on such place that one can reach it only after crossing 7-8 stairs. This keeps the base of the lift in level with the floor.
- The balcony and verandah in the shopping complex should be constructed in the north, east and north-east zone.
- Provisions for generator, electric motor and other electric appliances in the shopping complex should be made in the south-east zone.
- Overhead water tank of the shopping complex should be in the west direction.
- Offices and small shops of the shopping complex should be in the second floor or above. There must be a corridor, of an appropriate size, between the shops on every floor.

- The garden in the shopping complex should be laid in the north, east or north-east zone. Here a small temple could also be constructed, with entrance in north or east direction. Big trees should be planted in the south or west direction.
- The toilet could be constructed in the north-west zone, north or west direction of the complex. Toilet should never be constructed in the north-east zone.

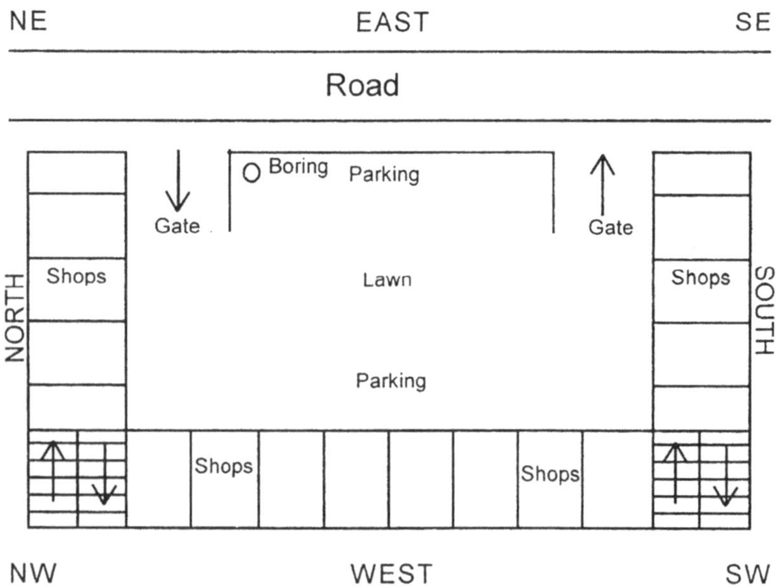

Commercial complex of "U" shape as per Vaastu

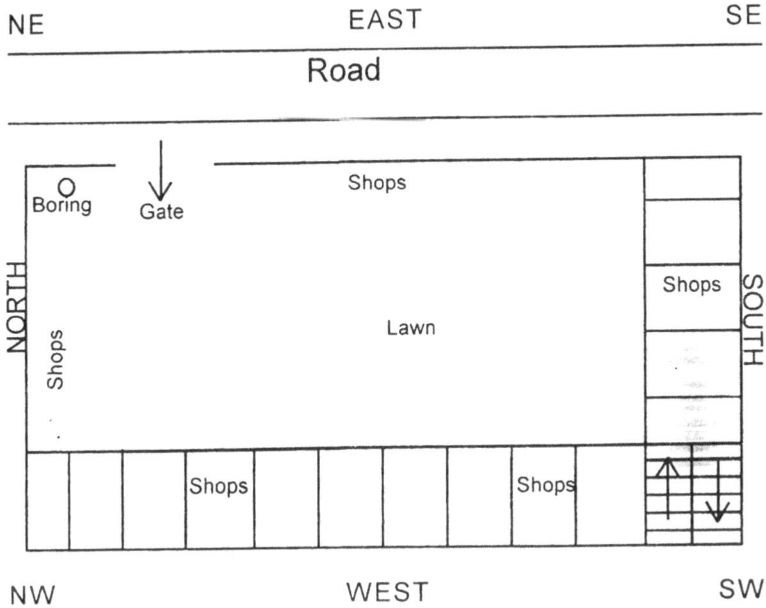

Commercial complex of "L" shape as per Vaastu

- Ample space should be left to parking car, scooters and cycles etc. in the north, east and north-east zone. The same direction is to be used for parking place if it is to be constructed in the basement. Basement should never be constructed in the south, west, south-west zone and centre.
- The building should be constructed in the south, west and east or south, west and north, while constructing "U" shaped shopping complex. Either north or the east direction of the same should be kept open, i. e. without construction.
- An "L" shaped shopping complex is as per Vaastu only if it is constructed in the south and west direction.
- Main entrance of the shopping complex should be in the east of the north-east zone, south of the south-east zone, west of the south-west zone or north of the north-east zone. It should never be constructed in the east of the south-east zone, south of the south-west zone or north of the north-west zone.

HOTEL AND VAASTU

Every body wishes to enjoy beautiful scenes of waves of water colliding with the sea shore, hills touching to the sky, boastingly flowing rivers, beautiful gardens, dense forests etc. One has to move away from home, to some tourist place, to enjoy them. For business purpose also, in addition to tourism, one has to move away from home. While at new places people stay in hotels eat there, move around and finish their work. It is human nature that while away from home, we want comfort and eatables just like home.

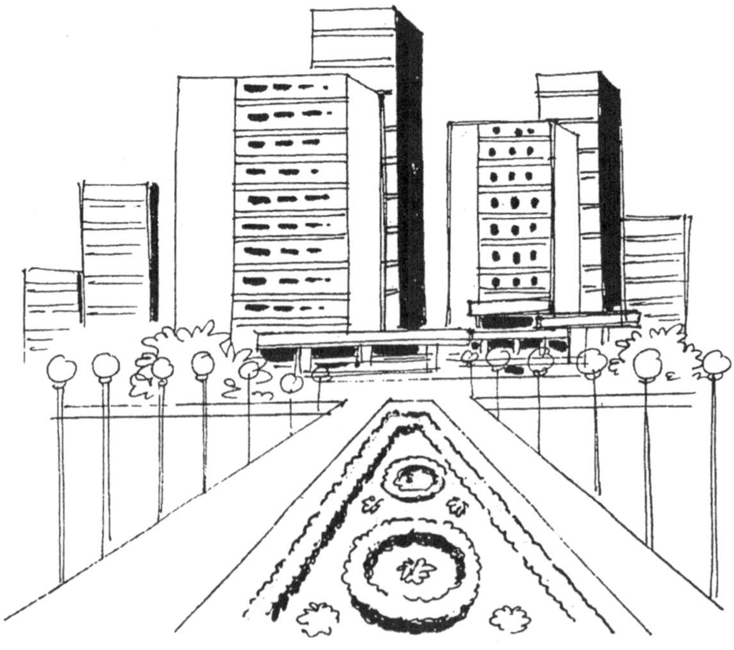

To create a home away from home, hotels are bright in such a way that all types of amenities are available to their customers. That's why it costs a lot to construct a hotel.

If a hotel is constructed as per Vaastu then it is airy, full of water and sunlight. This makes the atmosphere cheerful and beautiful. Guests staying in such hotels feel comfortable. Rooms in such hotels are always fully occupied. One has to wait to get place in the restaurants of such hotels. The hotel owner earns good. Employees of such hotels get attractive salaries. They serve the guests of the hotel properly, whereas if a hotel is not constructed as per Vaastu then nobody likes to go and stay there. If somebody stays there he wants to leave soon, as he does not feel comfortable there. Employees also do not work for long and other problems also add on. In such circumstances the owner has to recur heavy losses and finally he closes the hotel. Most of the big hotels of India have not been constructed as per Vaastu and are running in losses.

If following Vaastu principles are taken care of, while constructing a hotel, the owner will earn good profit and the guests staying there will also be happy:

- The plot, on which the hotel is to be constructed, should be square or rectangular in shape for good financial gains. This should not be of irregular shape. The south-west corner of the plot should be of 90^0. Lot of open space should left in the north and east while constructing a hotel.
- Cut, depressed and round north, east and north-east zone of the plot for hotel are inauspicious. These create problems for the owner. While it is auspicious to have these directions big, if these directions of the plot of hotel are cut, rounded or depressed then they should be corrected either by reducing or by increasing plot size. They should be made right-angled to avoid the bad effects.
- Underground water sources, e.g. well, bore-well and water tank should be in the north-east zone. If underground water source is in any other direction then

it is inauspicious. Swimming pool in the hotel should be constructed in the north or east direction. Construction of the swimming pool in the centre of the hotel causes tremendous financial problems.

- Construct "L" or "U" shaped hotels in the south, west or south-west zone only so as to provide more open space in the north and east direction.
- It is auspicious to construct main entrance of the hotel, in the east and south facing plots to the left while in the west and north facing plots it should be in the right-hand side. The passage to enter and exit the hotel, doors of all the rooms and entrance of the restaurant should be as per the figure.
- Electricity meter, transformer, generator and other electrical appliances should be kept in the south-east zone.
- The air conditioning plant, in case of centrally air conditioning, should be placed in the south-west zone. If individual air conditioning is to be done then the air conditioner can be put anywhere except on the north, east and north-east zone.
- The pantry of the hotel should be constructed in the south-east zone where ample light and air is available. Mixer, grinder etc. should be kept on a platform in the south direction. Tandoor, hearth, microwave oven etc. should be kept in the south-east zone. The store of the kitchen can be in the south of the south-west or west and all the groceries can be put here.
- Barbeque and campfire should be done in the south-east zone. It should never be done in the east of the southeast. It can be done in the south of the south-east if the swimming pool is in the east. Geyser should be kept in the south-east zone.
- Overhead water tank could be constructed anywhere from the west of the north-west to south of the south-west.
- Septic tank should only be constructed in the east or north

direction only. If the swimming pool is in anyone of these directions, then it should be shifted to other direction.

- Health club, massage room and steam bathroom etc. of the hotel should be constructed in the north-west zone. Indoor games can also be arranged near this place.
- Common hall or the conference room for the recreation of the guests of the hotel should be constructed in the south-west zone. Play ground for the children or garden should be constructed in the east or north direction.
- Basement should be constructed in the north, east or the north-east zone of the hotel. Basement constructed in any other direction than these produces many problems.
- Basement of the hotel should be used only for restaurant, casino, nightclub and bar etc.
- The basement could also be used for the meetings, exhibitions and shopping arcade etc.
- Vehicle parking of the hotel could be constructed in the south or west direction. The basement could also be used for this purpose.
- Garden can be created around the hotel but care should be taken to plant small trees in the north and east and bigger ones in the south and west directions.
- Lift in the hotel should be in the north or east direction. If a 6-7 ft. pit is dug for the lift in direction other than the east or north, then this can cause tremendous loss. If the lift is to be kept in direction other than the north and east then it should be placed 5-6 steps above the ground level so as to avoid a pit. A clockwise staircase in any direction other than the north-east zone could be constructed to go upstairs. The lift and staircase should never be put in the north-east zone.

RECEPTION OF THE HOTEL

- The reception of the hotel should be on the ground floor near the entrance. The receptionist should sit facing either east or north.
- The cash counter of the hotel should be kept in the south or west direction of the reception in such a way that cash box should open either in the north or east direction.
- TV, cable and intercom control box of the hotel should be kept in the south direction of the reception.
- The cloakroom of the hotel should be in the north-west zone of the reception.
- The administrative office of the hotel could be constructed in the south or west of the hotel.

ROOMS OF THE HOTEL

Special attention should be paid to construct and decorate the rooms of the hotel. These rooms are for the guests who stay there. The hotel is constructed for them and by their presence the hotel runs.

- Beds in the rooms should be kept in such a way that head is in the south and legs are in the north while sleeping. There should not be any beam or loft above the bed.
- No toilet or bathroom should be constructed in the north-east zone of the room.
- Air conditioner could be placed on any wall other than in the north, east or the north-east zone.
- Walls of the room should be painted with light colour only. Dark shades should never be used. These produce aggression.
- Safe in the room should be kept in the west, south or south-west zone. Sofa and coffee table can be put in the north or east direction.
- Heater to keep the room warm should be placed in the south of the south-east zone. The geyser in the bathroom should be placed in the south-east zone.

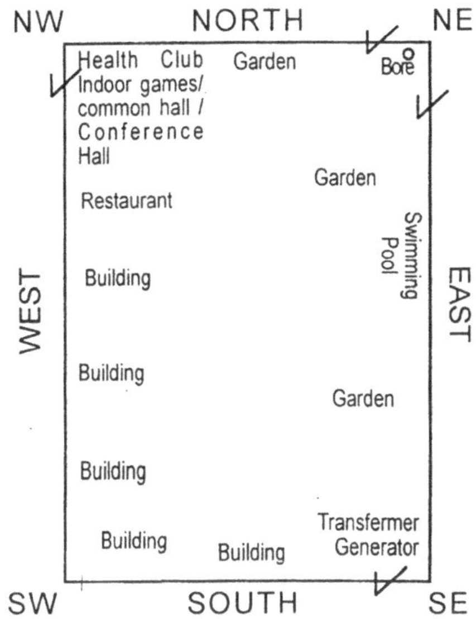

Map of the hotel as per Vaastu

RESTAURANT IN THE HOTEL

Restaurants are constructed to provide food to the guests staying in the hotel. It should be in the west direction of the hotel. The In-charge of the restaurant should sit on a chair facing east or north, in such a way that he can see every customer sitting in the restaurant.

TOWNSHIP AND VAASTU

In every big city nowadays new townships are being developed to make everyone's dream of having a house, true. Every type of modern amenity such as, shopping mall, school, hospital, banquet hall, multiplex, bank, swimming pool and garden etc. are available in these townships along with the security. Plots, flats, duplex, penthouse, bungalows, shops etc. are available in these townships for every income group.

Recently Shri Manoj Sherawat, from Gurgaon wanted to purchase a flat, constructed as per the Vaastu principles, where he could live with his family happily.

For this purpose, he took me to an upcoming township of Gurgaon on the Jaipur road, where he wanted to purchase a flat. I saw township and flats being constructed there. After observing the whole township as per Vaastu, I told him that the same was being developed on plot which was not as per the Vaastu principles. The plot had a cut in north-east zone. The main entrance of the township was being constructed in the north of the north-west. Two roads have been developed in the back portion of the township, one towards west of the south-west and another towards south of the south-west. In addition, the south of the south-west of this township was also protruded. All these are very significant Vaastu defects and due to these this township would not be able to attract many people. This township would lack activity and silence would prevail everywhere. There would be disputes between its builder and those investing here. Due to all these defects the lives of all those living here would not be happy. The builders developing this township would have to incur heavy losses no matter how big and experienced they might be. Thus I advised him not to invest there.

After listening Shri Manoj informed me that for the last one and half year the developers had been advertising through news papers and City cable, every time coming with some extra attraction for the investors, but in vain. Till date they could get only 10% booking with difficulty. Otherwise when the same builder develops anything, anywhere people make long queues for bookings after the very first announcement of the project. This project is being developed with very slow speed.

We were attracted to this project due to some very attractive offers, made to us by the builder. Now, after listening to you we think that due to these Vaastu defects only the flats of the township are not being sold. That's why the builder is making such attractive offers for the bookings, whereas in any other projects he does not make such attractive offers.

Mostly the builders do not follow the basic Vaastu principles, while finalizing a plot for their projects. This negligence costs them low profits and sometimes they are completely ruined financially. Hence the builders should follow the following Vaastu principles while purchasing plot or land for the construction of a multi-storeyed building to attract many people who may live there happily and the builder gets good profit.

- Develop township on such a plot, which has deep pits, ponds and river etc. in its north-east zone and higher hillocks and mound in the south-west zone. Such a place will be a boon for the fame and prosperity of the township.

- The shape of the plot, on which the township is to be developed, should be square or rectangular for excellent financial gains. Township should never be developed on a plot of irregular shape.
- Cut, depressed and round north, east and north-east zone of the plot of township are inauspicious. They create a lot of problems for the builder. On the contrary, if these directions are big then it is auspicious. If these directions are inauspicious due their shape they should be corrected by some adjustments to avoid any bad effects.
- The north, east and north-east zone of the plot should be lower than the south, west and south-west zone for success of the township. Higher north, east and north-east zone of the plot invites the ill fate. If the north-east zone, north and east directions are higher then the soil of them should be transferred to the south-west zone, south and west before construction starts.
- All the roads of the township should be parallel from east to west or north to south to facilitate the construction of the buildings in rectangle or square-shaped plots.
- Main entrance of the township and other doors should be kept in the east of the north-east, south of the south-east, west of the north-west or north of the north-east. They should never be kept in the east of the south-east, south of the south-west, west of the south-west or north of the north-west. All these principles are applicable to all the flats and offices etc. also to be constructed in the township.
- Construction of any type of pit like swimming pool, artificial water fall, pond, well and borewell, in the township, should be done in the north, east or north-east zone only. It is inauspicious to construct them in any other direction. Any type of pit in the centre of the township creates tremendous financial problems.
- The rainwater of the township should flow towards east, north or north-east zone. The drainage water of the

township should also flow out from north or east direction.

- Water storage tank could be constructed in the south or south-west zone of the plot.
- The arrangement for the electricity meter, transformer, generator and other electrical appliances should be done in the south-east zone only.
- Higher buildings of the township should be constructed in the south, west and south-west zone. Medium buildings should be constructed in the south-east and north-west zone. The lowest buildings should be constructed in the north and east directions.
- Maximum open space should be left in the north and east direction of the township. Temple, meditation centre and garden etc. should be constructed in the east or north-east zone of the township, for good health. This way the residents of the township will be able to get maximum benefit of the vital morning sun rays.
- Construction of water park should be done in the north of the north-east, amusement park, multiplex, banquet hall, health club should be done in the centre of the north and other clubs should be constructed in the north-west zone of the township.
- If the education centre, hospital, banks and shopping malls of the township are to be constructed small then they should be in the east and if they are to be constructed big, then they should be in the south or west direction.
- Any building in the township such as, multi-storeyed flats, shopping malls, schools, hospitals, banks and clubs etc. should be constructed in the rectangle or square shape only. The flats or rooms to be constructed in them should also be of the same shape.
- There should not be any bathroom in the northeast zone of the township.
- Basement or under ground parking in the township should be in the north or north-east zone only.

GURGAON – BEAUTIFUL EXAMPLE OF IDEAL VAASTU

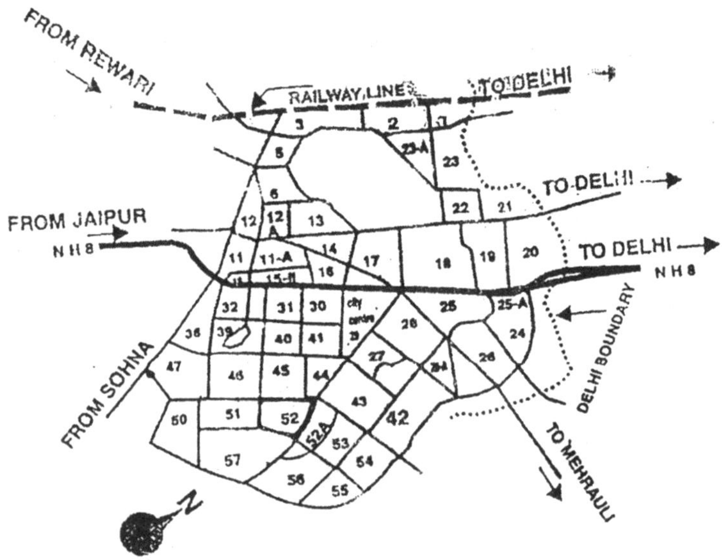

The business of the outsourcing is increasing with tremendous speed in the whole world. Many renowned companies of western countries, USA and Japan, which are far ahead due to their industrial revolution, get their jobs done here in India. Many commercial institutes situated in the Gurgaon, a city south to Delhi, do a very big part of this outsourcing business in India. This place is the centre of various activities due to opening of corporate offices of many foreign companies. Due to IT offices and call centers the significance of the city of Gurgaon has increased manifold. Gurgaon is getting good name due to all these activities, in the whole world.

Gurgaon is developing fast as a commercial centre of India and is now internationally renowned. Due to this new shopping malls, multiplexes, skyscrapers and townships with all the modern facilities are coming up daily in this city. Vaastu has played a very significant role in the fame and prosperity of Gurgaon, which attracts people from all over the world. The situation of Gurgaon is exactly as per the Vaastu principles. As per the Vaastu principles the southern part of any village, city or state is wealthier, that always has glamour and lustre.

Due to population explosion Delhi is expanding in all the directions. That's why all the cities surrounding Delhi, such as Ghaziabad, Sahibabad, Faridabad, Noida and Gurgaon are developing fast. Ghaziabad is situated in the east of Delhi and west of UP. Noida is situated in the west of UP and in the east of the southeast of Delhi. And Faridabad is situated in the south of the south-east of Haryana and Delhi, whereas Gurgaon is situated in the south of Delhi and Haryana state. In addition to this the slope of the land here, especially in the direction of Delhi, is from south to north direction. That's why Gurgaon is developing faster as compared to other cities around Delhi. This fast pace of Gurgaon will continue due to its Vaastu in future too.

The development of a city starts from one point and continues in all the directions. In this course the southern part always develops more and centre of the north-east zone gradually loses its glamour. On the other hand the region of the city from the centre of the south to south-west zone gains more grandeur. All the other directions develop with normal pace.

Gurgaon has been developed on the basis of sectors. There are 57 sectors in Gurgaon, at present. Sector nos. 24, 25, 25A and 26 fall in the north-east zone. This part of the city will lag behind in development and will become a place of the poorest in future. The development of the sector nos. 16, 11, 11A, 15, 30, 31 and 32 will be fast because they are in the south-west zone. There will be skyscrappers, shopping malls, multiplexes, amusement parks and townships with best amenities in this part. These sectors will have glamour and their fame and prosperity will keep on increasing. These sectors will possess more grandeur than other sectors. Sector nos. 44, 45, 46, 47, 50, 51, 52 and 57, which are in the south will also develop fast. Prosperity and grandeur will be visible in these sectors too. All other sectors in south-west zone will develop at a normal pace. On the other hand sector nos. 26A, 28, 27, and 42; situated in the east and 18, 19, 20, 21 and 22, situated in the north will develop extremely slowly.

On the basis of above analysis, based on the Vaastu principles, we can assume that the prices of the property in the south and south-west zone of Gurgaon will shoot up due to fast development. Those who wish to invest there for a prosperous life and successful business should invest in the plots that are developed as per the Vaastu principles.

VAASTU PROBLEMS AND SOLUTIONS

I receive mail of readers as I write on Vaastu in the famous Indian magazine *'Grihlaxmi'*. I have described the problems and solutions of some of them below. You can look to the Vaastu of your commercial place and houses and get the solutions of the problems by reading these.

SPECIAL: Most of the readers usually describe the length, breadth, main entrance, windows, drawing room, kitchen, toilet, bathroom, underground water source etc. while sending the map. A few describe the floor level of the place in their letters. This should never be ignored while doing Vaastu analysis.

PROBLEM: I regularly read your articles in the magazine *'Grihlakshmi'*. I am going to purchase a new flat. Please look at the map and let me know where and what type of changes should I make? Please let me know about decoration too. I think the north-east zone of the flat is cut.

–Sadhna Singh, Jamshedpur, Bihar

SOLUTION: There is no indication for the directions in your map. It is difficult to advise you without the knowledge of the directions.

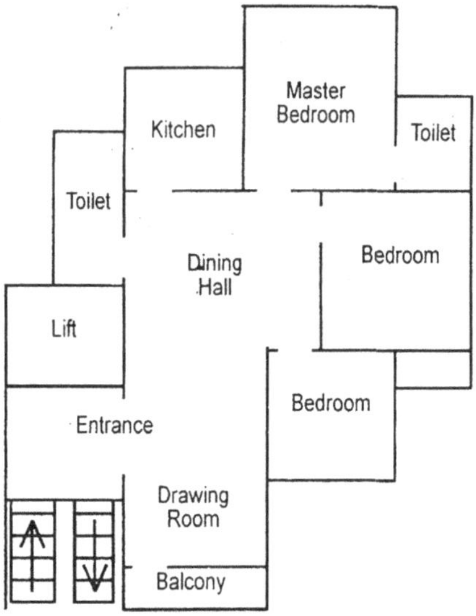

Map of flat of Sadhna Singh

You have written about cut northeast zone of the flat. Cut north-east zone of any building, whether residence, office, flat, temple, shop or hotel is inauspicious. The residents of such places always suffer from physical, mental and financial problems. I am of the opinion that this is a completely irregular shaped flat. I suggest you not to purchase the same because it will not be auspicious.

PROBLEM: I want to purchase this flat. How is the Vaastu of the same? How should I arrange the household things in this flat? Kindly guide me and give your valuable suggestions.

–Ms. Urmila Khatri, Delhi

SOLUTION: You have sent the map of the flat that is of irregular shape and has cut north-east zone. This gives financial, physical and mental problems to the residents.

The south-west of this flat is protruded, due to construction of toilet, which will create problems for the males of the house especially.

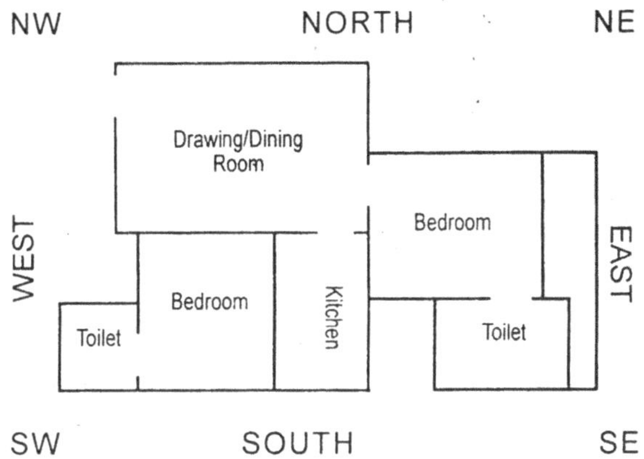

Map of the house of Ms. Urmila Khatri

After looking carefully the map of this flat I suggest you that if you are comfortable in your present residence then please do not shift into the new one. This will be a wise decision.

PROBLEM: I read your article "When you purchase flat", in the magazine '*Grihlaxmi*'. I studied my house, after reading your article. I found that for some conditions you had written, "don't ever do" or "inauspicious", these are present in our house. We did not give a thought to such things at the time of the construction of our house. We had two earning members in our house, earlier now we have none. My father died, after long sickness, untimely. Please suggest simple and economic ways for the prevention of Vaastu defects.

–Preetam Singh, Jaipur, Rajasthan

SOLUTION: Following Vaastu defects are the reasons of your problems:

There is a bore well in the north-west zone of your house. The financial loss is due to this borewell.

The north-east zone is covered due to the toilet and bathroom. This creates health problems and the money of the family is also flushed through this route.

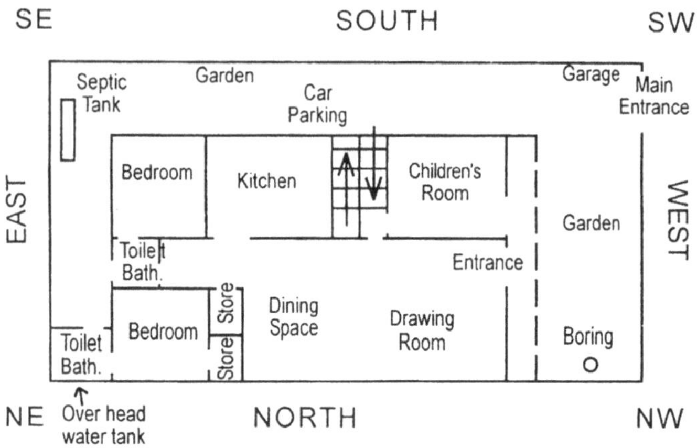

Map of the house of Mr. Preetam Singh

Main entrance of the house is in the west of the south-west zone, which gives financial, mental and physical problems to the male members of the house.

If the main entrance is in the south-west zone, north-east zone is covered, underground water source is in the north-west zone then the male member of that family dies untimely death. This happened with your father.

The south-west zone is more open than the north-east zone of the house. This is also inauspicious.

Please make following changes:

- Demolish the toilet bathroom of the north-east zone completely. Make an underground water source, such as borewell, well or tank on this place.
- Fill the borewell by soil completely. Make main entrance of the house in the west of the north-west zone.
- Construct a wall to completely close the entrance in the west of the south-west zone.
- Cover the south and west directions, which are open, by some construction or plantation.

I believe that these changes will bring relief and your life will be happy and simple.

PROBLEM: I have purchased a new flat and sending you the map of the same. Please give me proper guidance and solution after going through the lay out.

–Rakesh Kumar Sharma, New Delhi

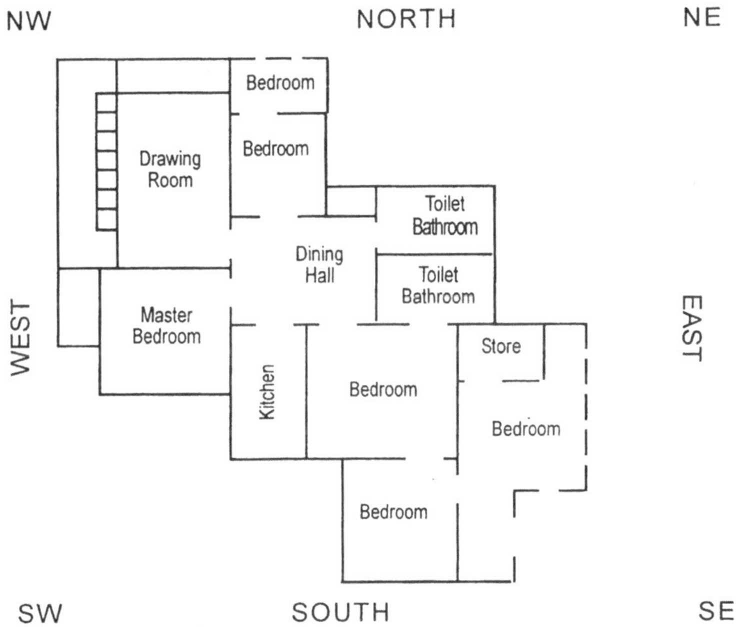

Map of the house of Mr. Rakesh Kumar Sharma

SOLUTION: There are several Vaastu defects in the lay out sent by you.

Your flat is constructed in an irregular shape. It has cut north-east zone. There are toilet and bathroom in the north-east zone. Cut, depressed or round north-east zone is inauspicious as per Vaastu. Money is flushed out of the house due to the toilet and bathroom in the north-east zone and someone is always ill in the house.

No alternative remedy is available in the Vaastushaastra or Feng Shui for this defect. It will be better that you do not shift in the flat and sell it.

PROBLEM: There is slow progress in the business, low margin of profit, always stuck in some kind of problem and have disturbed mental peace. If there is any Vaastu defect in the root of our problems, then please let us know. Please also suggest us the remedy.

–Manoj Ji, Jhansi (U.P.)

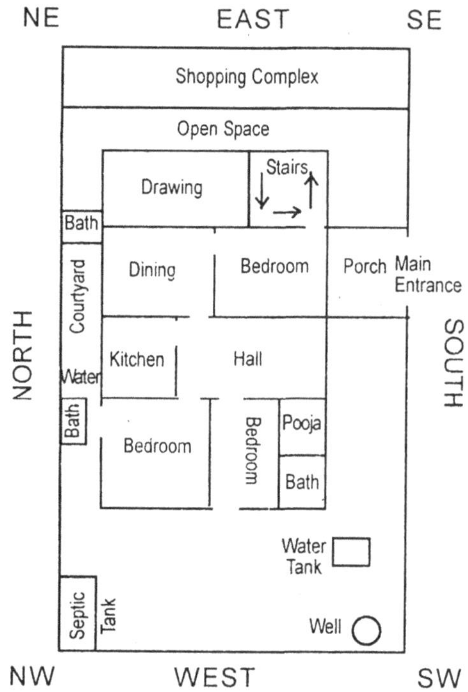

Map of house of Manoj Ji

SOLUTION: Well in the west of the south-west and water tank in the south are the causes of your problems.

Any kind of pit in the south direction creates all types of problems, such as, financial, mental and physical sufferings and sudden accidents etc. as per the Vaastu principles. Close both, well and water tank by soil filling first. Close the septic tank, situated in the west of the north-west zone, by soil filling and construct new one in the north direction, on the place where you have written *Aangan* (courtyard).

Due to no construction in the north-east zone, the north of your building is cut. It is a significant Vaastu defect. You could extend the drawing room till the bathroom in this direction or construct a small room and make it a temple to correct this defect. Constructing an underground water source in the open space of the north-east zone will be very useful.

These changes will cure almost 80% of your problems and your life will be simple, happy and better than before.

PROBLEM: It seems that we do not achieve even 50% success of what is our ability. Nobody has mental peace in the family. How can we progress and remain happy in this house? Will the extension of the house benefit us? The neighbour is ready to sell us his part. Please guide.

–Yashpal Singh Khanuja, Barwala, Haryana

SOLUTION: Following Vaastu defects are the reason of your problems:

Your house is of the staircase shape and the main entrance is in the south-east zone. East direction of the house is cut. All these are opposite to the Vaastu principles and are the reasons of the problems and obstruction in the progress of your family.

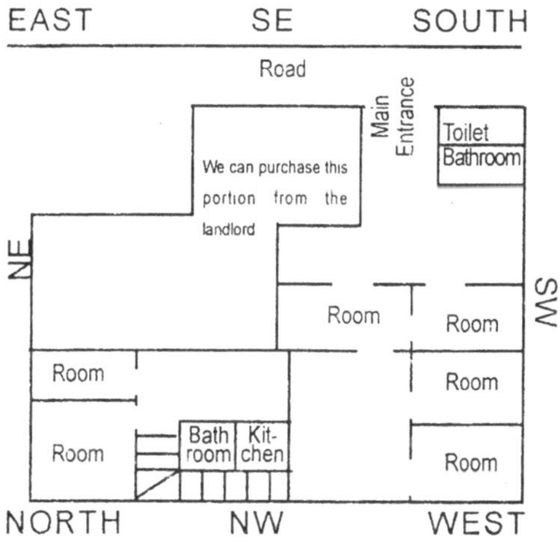

Map of the house of Yashpal Singh Khanuja

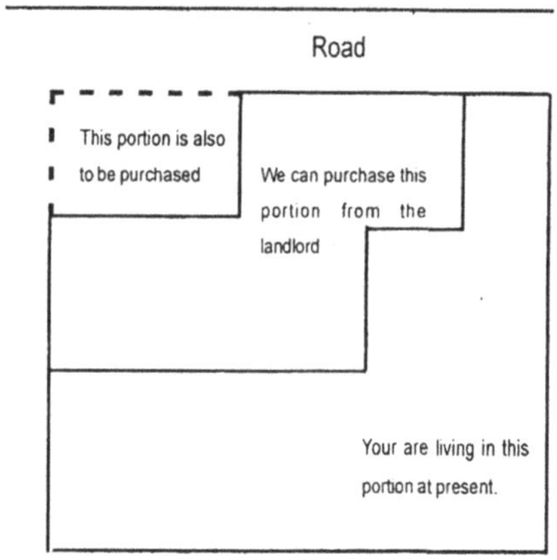

Corrected map

Extension of your house will not give any relief because the east direction will remain cut.

If you could add some part in the east, which is cut, as per the corrected map and construct your main entrance of the house on that added part then all your problems will be finished. If you cannot do this then, for your good future it will be better that you shift elsewhere from this house.

PROBLEM: I have a plot. I am thinking of constructing twin buildings on the same. I am sending here with the map. I request you to look this as per Vaastu and let me know if there is any significant defect.

–Sanjeev Kumar Agrawal, Farrukhabad (U.P.)

SOLUTION: A thorough study of your map for twin buildings reveals that the north-east zone of your plot is cut and south of the south-west is protruded. This has converted the plot into fan shape.

As per your map, the house is surrounded by one compound wall. Thus both the houses will have to be treated as one entity while ascertaining Vaastu. Main entrance is in the east of the south-east zone, as per the map. Toilet is in the center of the building. One kitchen is in the north and another in the south direction. All these are significant Vaastu defects.

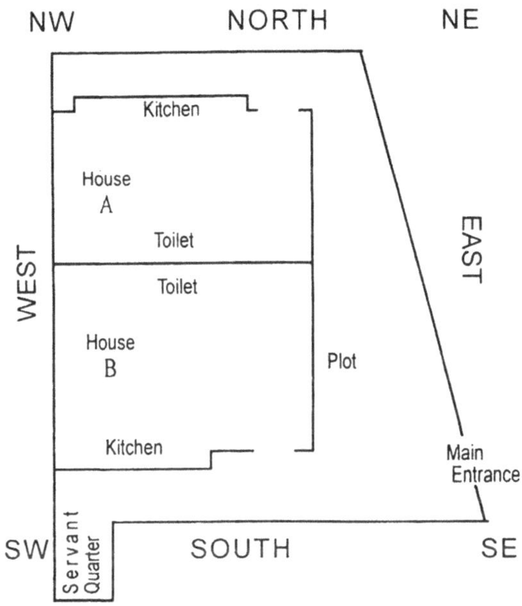

Map of house of Sanjeev Kumar Agrawal

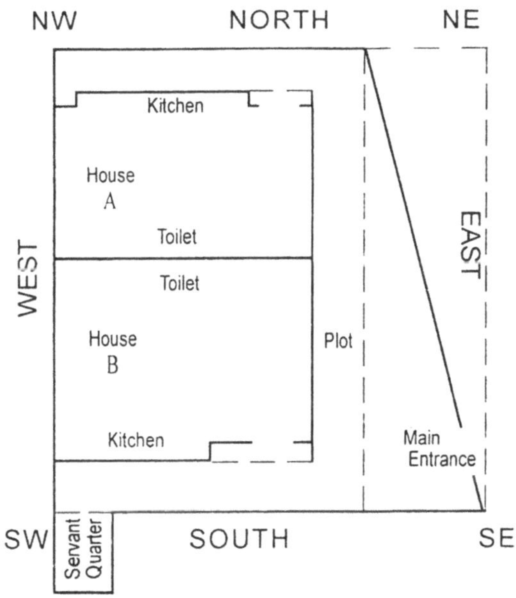

Corrected map

The lives of all the residents will be difficult, if the construction is done as per this plan. Families residing in these houses will suffer from financial, mental, physical and all types of problems. Sudden painful accidents may also occur.

First of all correct your plot as per the corrected map. Separate the protruded south of the south-west zone by a wall. Extend your compound wall in the east of the north-east zone or leave place in the east of the south-east zone to correct the same. Now construct the house as per Vaastu. Correct the cut in the east of the north-east zone and east of the south-east zone, as shown in the map.

You will have to sacrifice some place of the plot to construct as per Vaastu.

PROBLEM: I cannot save money or is spent unnecessarily and I face scarcity of money. I spend a lot on grains too. Is there a simple solution to this problem?

SOLUTION: I have read your letter and seen the map of your house. It has be following Vaastu defects:

Main entrance of the house and compound wall are constructed in the wrong place. All the doors of the house are also in the wrong places. Due to these defects there are disputes and quarrels in the house. Change the place of the doors and fix them at proper places, as per the corrected map.

South-east zone is the best place for the kitchen. Second preference is given to the west direction.

But the problem of this second preference is that this increases the consumption and misuse of the grains, which is applicable in your case too. In your kitchen, which is in the west direction, the housewife has to face south while preparing food. If you change this direction to east facing while preparing food, as per the corrected map, the prosperity of the house will increase.

In your house the open space is from east to west through south. It is inauspicious as per Vaastu. Separate this space by a wall, as suggested in the corrected map.

I believe that these changes will reduce the disputes and

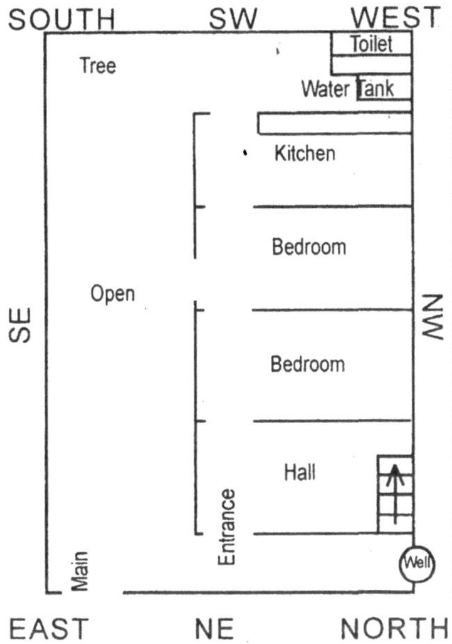

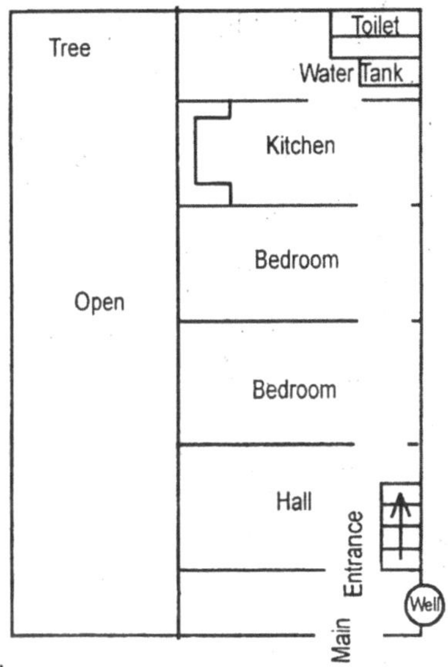

Map of the house of Vijay Patil *Corrected map*

quarrels in the house. You will have mental peace and financial condition will be improved.

PROBLEM: Please find enclosed here with a map of a flat I am going to purchase. Is it as per Vaastu or not? Should I purchase it or not?

–Niranjan Shah, Delhi

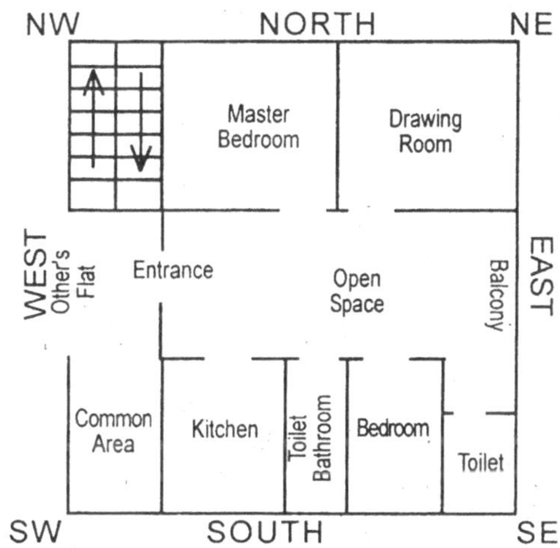

Map of the house of Niranjan Shah

SOLUTION: You have sent to me the map of a flat on the first floor. I have seen many flats in Delhi. Builders do not construct the flats as per Vaastu, as they want to make use of every inch of the space available. That's why 90% flats are not constructed as per the Vaastu principles. The map, which you have sent to me, is not 100% as per Vaastu but is quite good. There are a few such readymade flats, which are almost as per Vaastu principles. Hence this flat could be purchased as it is good as per Vaastu.

PROBLEM: I am sending the map of my flat. It is on rent. Is it as per Vaastu? Should I make some changes to it? We have shifted here 6-7 months back but since then I have lost my mental peace. Our financial condition is also as such since last 4-5 years. Please show us the right way.

–Smt. Vidya Agrawal, Chennai

SOLUTION: Your flat has only one major defect and that its kitchen is in the north direction. This has given you mental unrest.

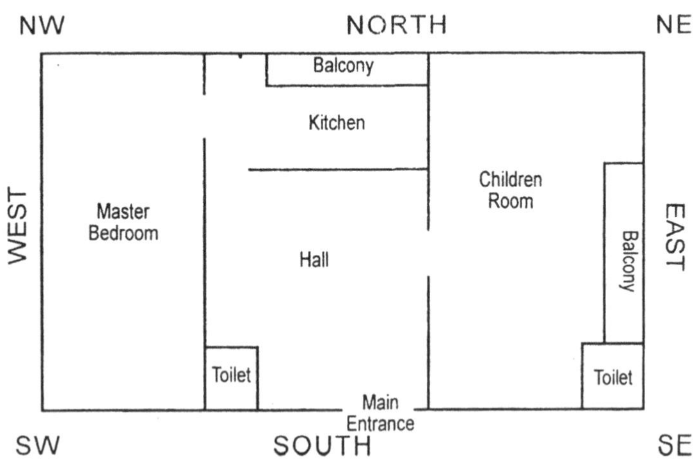

Map of the house of Smt. Vidya Agrawal

This rented flat is almost as per Vaastu. The bad financial condition could be due to your luck and not Vaastu of the flat.

PROBLEM: I had very good exports business. We are in trouble for the last one year when we shifted our office to this new building. Payments of the overseas are delayed and the government officials also tease. We are losing money too. Our routine office work is hampered due to absence of the female staff of the office as they are not well most of times. Please point out the problem in our building. Where should we put the generator for power production?

–Suman Sourav, Mumbai

SOLUTION: Following Vaastu defects are visible in your office as per the map sent by you, which are responsible for your problems:

The main entrance and the staircase are not in the right place. Remove them from the west and construct them in the north, as per the modified map.

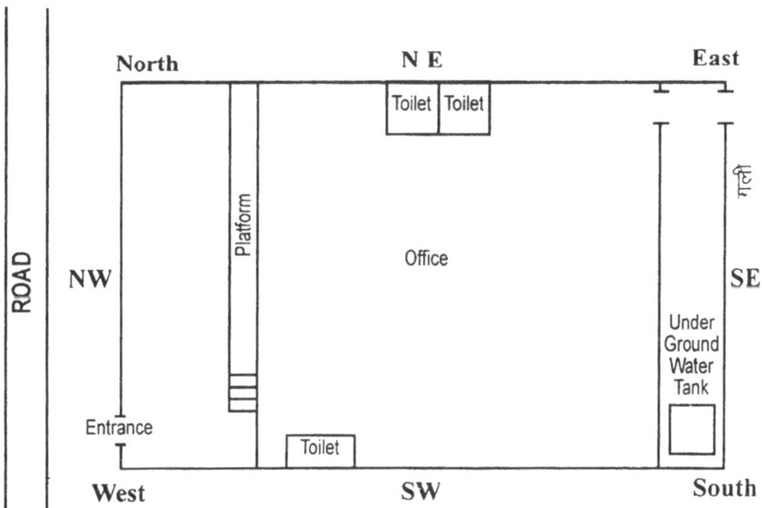

Map of the office of Suman Sourav

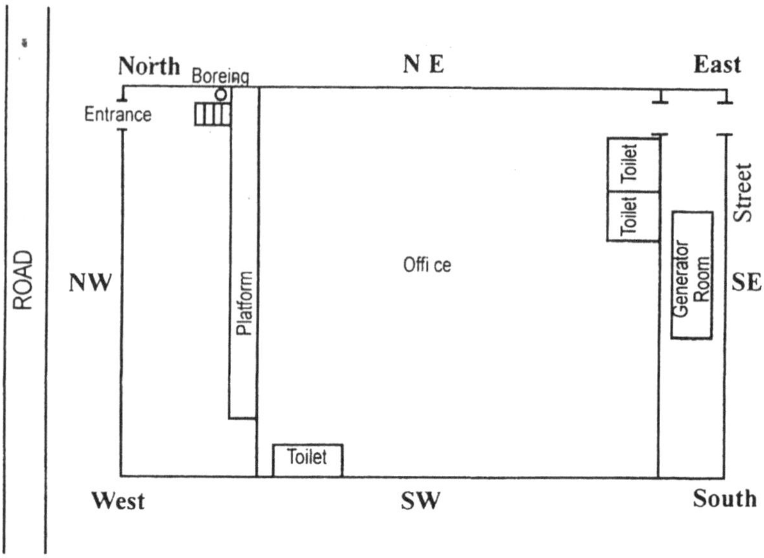

Modified map

One significant Vaastu defect is that the underground water tank is in the south. It affects the health of the women working in your office and causes the financial troubles. Due to this women seek leave often.

Get a new bore well dug in the north of the north-east zone and close this tank by soil filling as per the modified map.

Two toilets in the north-east zone cause health problems and flush the money out. Remove them from here and construct new one in the east. Put the generator in between the two walls in the southeast zone.

I hope that your life will be happy and simple after you make the corrections as suggested.

PROBLEM: We have office of our garment factory on the first floor of a multi-storeyed building. We are here for the last 8 months. We are in severe loss since we shifted here. Our staff is facing small accidents and getting quite a few injuries too. Is the Vaastu of our office bad?

–Ashok Kumar Varma, Delhi

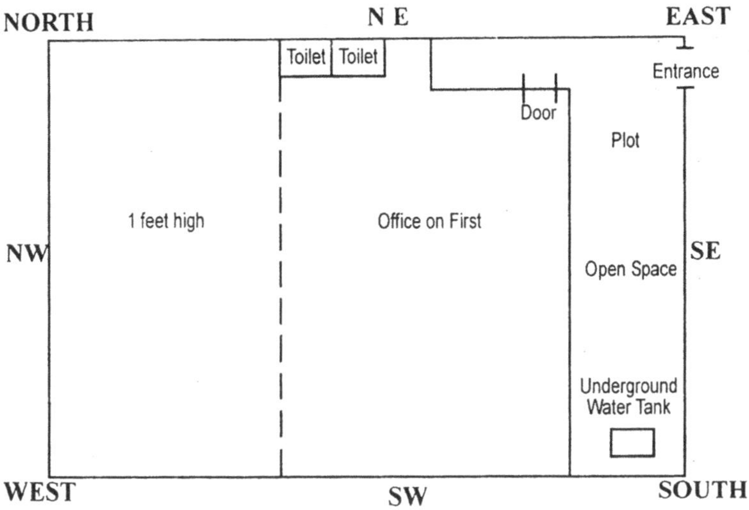

Map of Ashok Kumar Varma

SOLUTION: The portion from the north-east zone to north-west zone and almost half of the south-west zone of your office is approximately one foot high.

There is an underground water tank in south direction on the ground floor.

There are two toilets in the north-east zone of your office.

East direction and north-east zone of the office are cut.

All your problems are due to these Vaastu defects. Money is flushed out due to toilets in the north-east zone. Different troubles come due to cut in the east direction and north-east zone of the flat.

Water tank in south and 1-foot high portion of the flat of the office are the causes for the loss of money and accidents. This is exactly happening with you.

Flats of the multi-storeyed buildings are constructed on the columns and beams. Hence it is impossible to shift the main entrance and sewerage pipe. That's why it is impossible to demolish something in the flats. Hence to avoid the consequences of the bad effects of Vaastu defects, for you it will be better to leave this flat at the earliest.

PROBLEM: I am sending you the map of my flat. We have purchased this flat two years back and shifted here. The life has become troubled since we shifted here. We have incurred loss due to fire once. We are heavily indebted due to unnecessary expenditure. My job is also under threat. Please suggest if there is any defect in my flat.

–Parul Sharma, Sahibabad (U.P.)

SOLUTION: The following Vaastu defects are the reason behind all your problems:

The basement in the centre of your multi-storeyed building is affecting the financial position of all those who are living above in the flats.

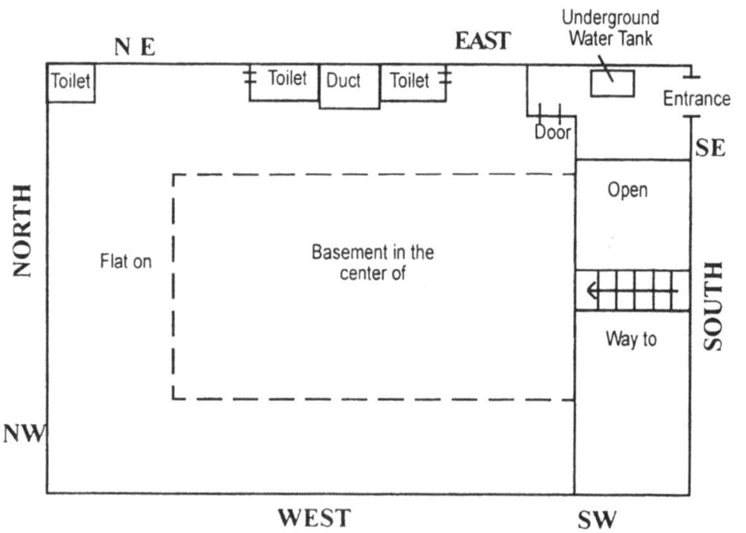

Map of flat of Parul Sharma

There is underground water tank in the south-east zone. This tank in the south-east zone is the cause for fire many times.

There are two toilets in the north-east zone, which are flushing money out. The east of your flat is cut due to a duct in the centre of the two toilets. These all are significant Vaastu defects, which cannot be corrected without demolition.

As the flats of a multi-storeyed building are constructed on the columns and beams, it is not easy and possible to shift or change the position of the main entrance, toilets, bathroom and sewerage pipe. I advice you to shift another flat which is constructed as per Vaastu. This would be a good decision for your future.

PROBLEM: We have started a call center one and a half years back, but have not got the desired success yet. We are still investing in it in spite of earning. Disputes between the partners have also started. Please give us proper suggestion.

–Abhay Thukral, Delhi

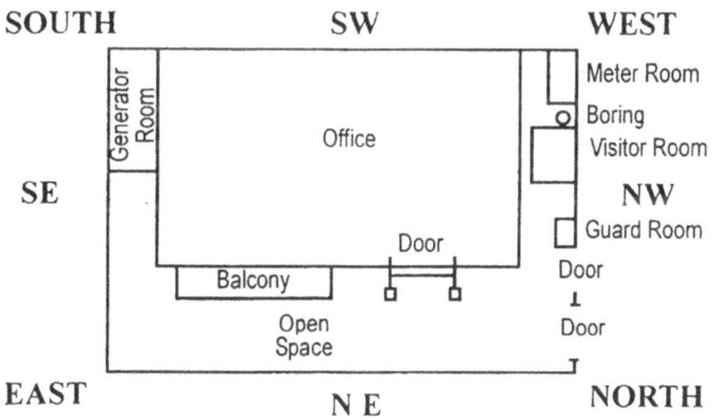

Map of the call center of Abhay Thukral

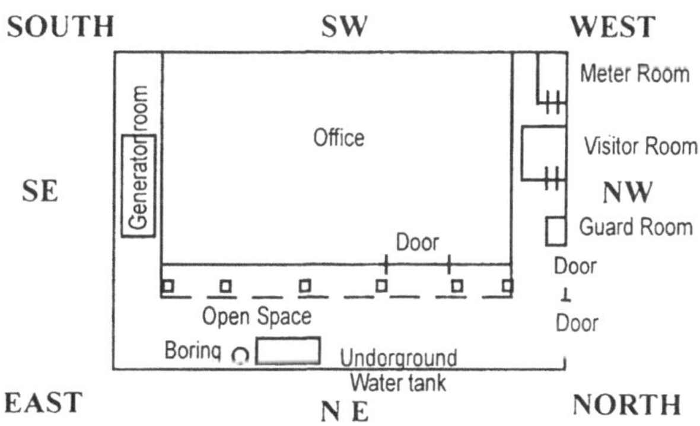

Modified map

SOLUTION: following Vaastu defects are present in your call center. Correct them as per the modified map and you will get benefit certainly:

- There is a bore-well in west of the north-west of your center. It is the cause for the dispute. Close it and construct in the east of the northeast zone.
- Construct the underground water tank too in the east of the north-east zone.
- There is a generator room in the tin shed in the south direction. Make some changes in it as per the modified map. North direction of the building protruded due to one step and two columns in the main entrance in north direction. This has increased the north-east zone. So demolish the step and construct four more columns similar to two columns already there. This will facilitate the construction of the balcony in full length.

SOLUTIONS TO VAASTU QUERIES

Q.1 : Is Vaastushaastra for the followers of Hinduism?

Ans. : No. The Indian *rishis* and *munis* invented Vaastushaastra for all those living on the earth. It is equally applicable to all belonging to any religion, cult or breed.

Q.2 : The earth encircles the sun and spins on its own axis, i.e. it is not stable. What is the utility of Vaastu in such a condition?

Ans. : It is right that the earth revolves on its axis and encircles the sun too. Our whole universe is also running towards infinite in the Milky Way very fast. Many carriages of a train run on the rail simultaneously. All the luggage in the carriages is stable while they are in motion. If suddenly the speed is either reduced or increased the luggage is disturbed. Similarly, the earth is also revolving on its axis with a uniform speed from the beginning. All the fixed things on its surface are stable. The basis of the Vaastushaastra is omnipresent five elements, viz. earth, water, fire, air and sky. To construct a house and decorate it as per these five elements is called Vaastu.

Q.3 : How does a layman know whether his house is as per Vaastu or not?

Ans. : Suppose your life is smooth, peaceful and business is good. When you change the residence and life becomes miserable, peace is disturbed, loss in business, face health problems then it clearly suggests that the new house or renovation of old one is not as per Vaastu.

Q-4 : If in spite of Vaastu defects life is happy and peaceful even than the removal of Vaastu defects is required?

Ans. : No. It is true that when the fortune is favourable and strong Vaastu defects are not felt. But when the fortune is not favourable then Vaastu defects become strong and disrupt the life. As long as fortune is favourable there is no need to make any changes in Vaastu. We visit our doctor only when we fall ill. A healthy person does not go to see his doctor. When day to day life is disturbed then only the removal of the Vaastu defects should be done.

Q-5 : Does Vaastu affect men and women separately?

Ans. : Yes. As per Vaastu east of the north east, north of the north-east, west of the north-west and west of the south-west represent region of man. South-east, south, south of the south-west and north of the north-west represent woman. All the other directions of Vaastu affect them equally.

Q-6 : Do east-facing or north-facing plots are as per Vaastu?

Ans. : No. All the four directions are natural. Construction can be carried out facing any one direction as per Vaastu. But as per Vaastu much open space should be left in the north and east directions to get more advantage of morning vital sun rays. Less open space should be left in the south and west directions to avoid contact with the negative rays of the sun afternoon. That's why there is no ample parking space in front of the south and west facing houses. East and north-facing plots are therefore rated better.

Q-7 : Is Vaastu applicable to the residents of ground floor only?

Ans. : Residents of ground floor are affected by Vaastu 100% because this is related to the earth. Underground water source, gardens, main gate, high and low of the ground and shape of the ground are all on the earth. The effect of the earth on Vaastu decreases as the height increases. It is only 80 to 90% effective on 8th-9th floor approximate.

Q-8 : Can Vaastu defects be eradicated by the Chinese Vaastushaastra–Feng Shui?

Ans. : Yes. Principle of the Feng Shui says that if there is a problem there is solution. But it is applicable to eradicate very small Vaastu defects only.

Q-9 : What is the similarity between Indian Vaastushaastra and Chinese Feng Shui ?

Ans. : There are different systems of medicine, e.g. Ayurved, Allopathy, Homeopathy and Unani etc. with only one aim, i.e. to keep the human being healthy. Similarly, Indian Vaastushaastra and Feng Shui are the old art of coordinating between shape, proportion and direction of a building, its surroundings with the environment.

Q-10: Are the principles of Vaastushaastra and Feng Shui applicable in India and China only respectively?

Ans. : No. The principles of Vaastushaastra and Feng Shui are based on the sun rays and magnetic rays flowing on the earth, which are not affected by man-made borders of the countries.

Q-11: Can Vaasushaastra and Feng Shui both be applied simultaneously in one Vaastu?

Ans. : Yes. The simultaneous application of Vaastushaastra and Feng Shui is much advantageous. Both should be applied under the advice of experienced and learned Vaastu consultants.

Q-12: How does Vaastu affect more than one property of the same person?

Ans. : If a person owns more than one properties then the Vaastu of property he uses for his residence and business purposes affects his life. The property, which he has given to others, will affect its users. If a property, which is not in any use affects the owner only.

Q-13: How does Vaastu affect more than one business premises of the same person?

Ans. : If a businessman possesses more than one business premises, then he will enjoy all the advantages of the business premises which is as per Vaastu. But He will have to face the disadvantages of all the Vaastu defects present in other business premises.

Q-14: In our country houses are small. Maximum people live in such houses where one or two rooms are shared by all the family members. In such a case what should be the solution?

Ans. : It is auspicious to decorate a small house or one room house treating it as single Vaastu as per Vaastu, i.e in the south-east region of the room hearth should be kept, water should be kept in the north-east angle and almirah should be kept in the south-west zone.

Please read article entitled "Interior Decoration of One Room and Vaastu" in the book *"Interior Decoration Vaastu and Feng Shui"* by this author.

Q-15: Young family member goes out of the house, in other city to study. Will the Vaastu defects of his house affect his career?

Ans. : No. Wherever that young person lives in other city the Vaastu of that place or room will affect his career.

Q-16: Does tying a cow or planting *tulsi* in front of the house eradicate Vaastu defects?

Ans. : Not at all. Due to its utility the cow is treated as mother. To tie cow, to apply the cow dung on the courtyard and to wash the house with cow urine are all our religious faiths. Similarly, due to its medicinal properties *tulsi* is worshipped. This is also our religious faith. Vaastushaastra is a science. Hence there is no advantage in applying any religious faith to eradicate Vaastu defects.

Q-17: In a house constructed as per Vaastu, can Vaastu defect originate per se?

Ans. : Many changes occur around us on their own. These sometimes create Vaastu defects even in a house constructed as per Vaastu. For example, small plants in the north-east zone of a house when grow become big trees then they start obstructing vital morning sun rays. It becomes a significant Vaastu defect.

If a highway or a bridge is constructed in the north or east and a big drain is constructed in the south or west of the house it creates a Vaastu defect. So there are many factors that may create Vaastu defect in a house constructed as per Vaastu.

Q-18: Is there any use of erecting Vaastu defect prevention machine?

Ans. : Not at all. There is no mention of any such machine in any book published on Vaastushaastra from the first book to any book till 1995. This Vaastu defects prevention machine has been invented by some greedy Vaastu consultants to plunder innocent people. It is created by charging very high price. It does not give even 1% relief.

Q-19: Is there any machine available to scarch Vaastu defects?

Ans. : No. The *rishi-munis*, who invented Vaastushaastra did not create such a machine. There is no description of such a machine in any old Indian or Chinese book. Some Vaastu consultants use "Lacquer Antenna" machine to detect Vaastu defects. By doing so they simply plunder people as this machine is basically used to measure energy of environment and human system.

Q-20: Can we eradicate Vaastu defects ourselves by merely reading a few books on the subject?

Ans. : No. Vaastushaastra seems very easy while reading but very difficult when applied. Only a few general Vaastu defects can be removed by reading some books but significant Vaastu defects can not be eradicated. People with shallow knowledge can not even differentiate between general and significant Vaastu defect. Hence it is recommended to consult an able and learned Vaastu consultant.

EPILOGUE

I have written 8 books on various aspects of Vaastu and Feng Shui, after gaining experience from successful Vaastu consultancy for years. I have written these books to facilitate you to construct or alter your residence or office as per Vaastu to lead a happy, peaceful and prosperous life.

I have experienced that in any corner of the world, if somebody is successful in any field of the life, his residence or office is as per Vaastu. If there is even a small Vaastu defect then that person has to suffer from the consequences of the same.

Common people have illusion that it is very costly to construct home as per Vaastu and its waste of space also. But it is completely wrong. In fact, it is very economical to construct home as per Vasstu and no space is wasted. Every inch of the space available is utilized in right ways. A small house, constructed as per Vaastu looks big and specious.

I have described various principles in my books to take full advantage of Vaastu. If you are unable, to follow them though I request you to follow only three important principles, as follows, to make your life happy and successful. These three principles are of significance as if they are compulsory question of 20 marks each in a question paper of 100 marks. All other principles bear only 1-2 marks. One point is to be made clear in this example that if there is anyone wrong answer the marking will then be negative.

1. North-east zone of any plot or building should never be covered, compressed, cut, deducted, or round. The south-west zone should not be raised.

2. Underground water source e.g. well, bore-well, tank, septic tank etc. or any other hole and any slope should only be in north, north-east or east direction. Never construct septic tank in north-east zone. It should be constructed in north or east direction only.
3. Boundary wall and main gate of the building can be in east of the north-east, south of the south-east, west of the north-west and north of the north-east.

Special

Under no circumstances the entrance gate should be in south of the south-west or west of the south-west.

If these three principles are followed, believe me, your Vaastu will be in grade I.

If in any building there is anyone of the above mentioned Vaastu defect then it is certain that the life of the residents will not be happy. Maybe due to strong fortune he may not feel the impact but the moment his fortune becomes weak, horrible problems will come in his life.

Above mentioned Vaastu defects can not be corrected with out destroying old construction. It is sheer waste of money and time to use pyramid, Shree Yantra, wind chime, crystal ball or other Feng Shui material, perform the *puja* for peace of Vaastu, stick craft, use *yantra, tantra* and *mantra* to correct these Vaastu defects.

Consult an able and experienced Vaastu consultant if you are suffering from Vaastu defects or want to construct a new building. Do not hesitate to pay proper fees to a good Vaastu consultant. I would like to draw your attention to the fact that a true and able consultant may charge high for his services. He gives you advice only and not pyramid, *yantra* or any other stuff. But the advantage of his advice is thousand times valuable than the fees you pay. Moreover, that advice makes your life happy, peaceful and prosperous.

THE NEBULA INTERNATIONAL SCHOOL OF SCIENTIFIC VAASTU

Vaastu Guru Mr. Kuldeep Saluja, an internationally renowned Vaastu consultant has written 8 books on different aspects of Vaastu and Feng Shui. He has been praised by his readers on international level and has become immensely popular.

Mr. Saluja has established an exclusive identity of his own by his deep study, thinking and research and knowledge of Vaastu, developed by the research work of *rishi* and *munis* for thousand years and Feng Shui a. five thousand year old Chinese Vaastu explored by the Chinese intellectuals. He has solved many doubts by question-answer sessions during his various trips to abroad. He is determined to create Vaastu education, students and teachers so as to reach this science to common people. To promote the course of this Vaastu education he has started a correspondence course. This correspondence course will give knowledge of Vaastu to all the keen students. They can take Vaastu as a career and earn money after becoming Vaastu consultants.

Many readers wrote to Mr. Saluja and showed their keen interest to learn Vaastu and to choose it as a career. Respecting this feeling "The Nebula International School of Scientific Vaastu" was established. A correspondence course of international level has been started by the institute. The curriculum has been prepared by Mr. Saluja on the basis of his experience (personal and practical) of 20 – 22 years. It has been prepared in such a way that it will unveil the scientific mysteries of Vaastu and you will be able to solve problems of others easily.

Mr. Saluja is confident that after finishing study of this course students will be able to eradicate Vaastu defects of house, shop, flat, office, marriage premises, factory, industry, farm house, agricultural land, multi-storeyed building and township etc. successfully anywhere in the world.

Correspondence course study material will be dispatched to the students by post. Evaluation of the assignments of the students will be done by Mr. Saluja. Minimum 75% marks are to be obtained. A practical workshop of all the successful students will be organized and the certificates will be distributed. Mr. Saluja will guide students about the practical aspects and other important information will be provided in this workshop. This course can be completed in minimum six to maximum twelve months.

PROCEDURE TO GET ADMISSION IN VAASTU & FENG SHUI COURSE

Those who are keen to take admission in this course, may apply giving their details e.g. name, address, phone no. etc. on a plain paper along with a D.D. of Rs.20000 as fee for the course. The D.D. should be in favour of "The Nebula International School of Scientific Vaastu" payable at Ujjain.

For the foreigners the fee is USD 1000.00. The fee is to be paid in one installment.

The application along with the D.D. can be sent at the following address:

The Nebula International
School of Scientific Vaastu
Billoo & Billoo, Freegunj, Ujjain-456010 (M.P.), India

You can contact on the following Nos. to get more information on the course.

Mobile : 09425091601
Phone : 0091-734-2513229, 2520068
Fax : 0091-734-2513842
e-mail : kuldeep@vaastuguru.com
billoo@sancharnet.in
website : www. vaastuguru.com
www.scientificvaastu.com

After the receipt of the application and fee, name will be registered for the course and identity card, syllabus and study material will be sent. The study material will be dispatched through courier from time to time.

VAASTU RELATED CONSULTATION WITH THE AUTHOR

Vaastu Guru Mr. Kuldeep Saluja is an experienced Vaastu consultant and the director of Billoo & Billoo group of business organization, a famous business organization of Ujjain.

It is generally observed that due to small Vaastu defects many construction works remain uncompleted or go through various problems during the course of construction. A family suffers financial, mental and physical problem or some accidents occur in the family, after shifting in a new house. A multi-storeyed building is ready for commercial use and is with all the modern amenities but nobody turns up to purchase. There are many problems in addition to these e.g. suddenly a good going business stops after expansion of shop or new furniture, shops of a new shopping complex are not sold and remain ruined, factory constructed and ready but production not started or production started but factory running in losses. Many such problems arise from time to time.

If you are also in trouble and desire to consult for removal of the Vaastu defects of house, shop, flat, office, marriage premises, factory, industry, farmhouse, agricultural land, shopping complex, multi-storeyed building or township etc. if you want to start a new construction as per Vaastu, then please contact at the following address and telephone no. and fix appointment.

Here it is worth mentioning that Mr. Saluja is a very busy Vaastu consultant. He very frequently visits many countries for Vaastu consultancy, in condition to India and is not easily available.

CONTACT AT

Kuldeep Saluja
The Nebula International School of Scientific Vaastu
Billoo & Billoo, Freeganj, Ujjain - 456 010, (M.P.), INDIA
Mobile : 094250 91601 **Phones :** 0091 - 734 - 2513229, 2520068
Fax : 0091 - 734 - 2513842
e-mail: kuldeep@vaastuguru.com
billoo@sancharnet.in
website : www.vaastuguru.com, www.scientificvaastu.com

Dear Readers,
This book is in your hands. How do you like it? There is every possibility of mistakes in the book. But our endeavour has been to give substantial information on Vaastu. Please do write to me about any mistake or suggestion. I would be highly obliged. I would like to correct it in the next edition. I will wait for your letters.

Kuldeep Saluja